BASIL AL-BAYATI

BASIL AL-BAYATI
RECENT WORKS

ACADEMY EDITIONS • ERNST & SOHN

Acknowledgement:

I would like to thank all of my friends for their effort and support over the years. I would also like to pay tribute to the generosity of my clients in their commissions for the buildings that gave me the opportunity to express myself in my art, and to fulfil my visions of architecture in these modern times.

To the members of my practice, artists, calligraphers and presentation team I likewise extend my thanks.

Many thanks also to the professional colleagues who have contributed their expertise to make many of my designs complete, and not forgetting the contractors, builders and craftsmen who make the dreams a reality.

Finally thanks to my publishers and their team.

Photographic Credits: Atlas Photography; Harrow Photolabs; Usama Al-Jawhari, p15; G Fehervari, p17.
Modelmakers: AG Modelmakers, p10, p81; Kevin Andrews, p81, p109; Thorpe Models, p12.
Perspectives: Brian Jennings, p83.

Cover: General plan of Oriental Village by the Sea, Dominican Republic
Page 2: Side elevation of Qasir Ghumdan Hotel, Sana'a, Yemen

First published in Great Britain in 1993 by
ACADEMY EDITIONS
An imprint of the Academy Group Ltd

ACADEMY GROUP LTD
42 Leinster Gardens, London W2 3AN
ERNST & SOHN
Hohenzollerndamm 170, 1000 Berlin 31
Members of the VCH Publishing Group

ISBN 1 85490 170 2 (HB)

Distributed to the trade in the United States of America by
ST MARTIN'S PRESS
175 Fifth Avenue, New York, NY 10010

Printed and bound in Singapore

CONTENTS

PARTIAL PLAN OF ORIENTAL VILLAGE BY THE SEA

FOREWORD

It is a great pleasure for me to be able to introduce the recent work of Basil Al-Bayati, an architect whose individuality and forceful imaginative work is on a level that few people have been able to achieve in the West. He has developed a unique way of approaching traditional problems, achieving a creative fusion of western and traditional methods in building.

Al-Bayati established his reputation as a symbolic architect with his early major religious building projects, particularly the Palm Mosque. But his exuberant nature is perhaps best expressed in his palaces in the Middle East and townhouses in the West.

A study of his architecture always reveals the hidden pattern that inspires each scheme whether it is symbolic, structural or fictional and whether he is building in the East or West. His work in England particularly, while revealing his obsession with the symbolism that inspires his buildings, expresses the joy of architecture and scrupulously respects the constraints imposed upon the site.

His recent work includes two projects in the Middle East: the Qasir Ghumdan Hotel in Yemen and the Sinmar Palaces, which take their inspiration from ancient stories celebrating buildings. Both draw on ancient mythology for their structural shapes and symbolism and tell the story of the rulers and peoples of the past who inhabited these great buildings.

Projects in England, including the College for Islamic Studies, Oxford, and the Edinburgh Mosque, take analogies from the traditional fabric surrounding the site, imbuing it with an Islamic spirit.

Also included is a competition project for a seaside development. Here Al-Bayati's solution is free form, organic architecture and hidden structures, but still incorporating a rigorous pattern.

Thus this volume, which includes work over the past four years, presents a wide range of projects in which Al-Bayati applies his own solutions to each and every one. It is modern architecture at its most individual, aiming at reconciling two almost irreconcilable worlds. When the fusion is achieved, as in the Edinburgh mosque, the result is a vivid, clear architecture with its own unique identity.

Andreas Papadakis

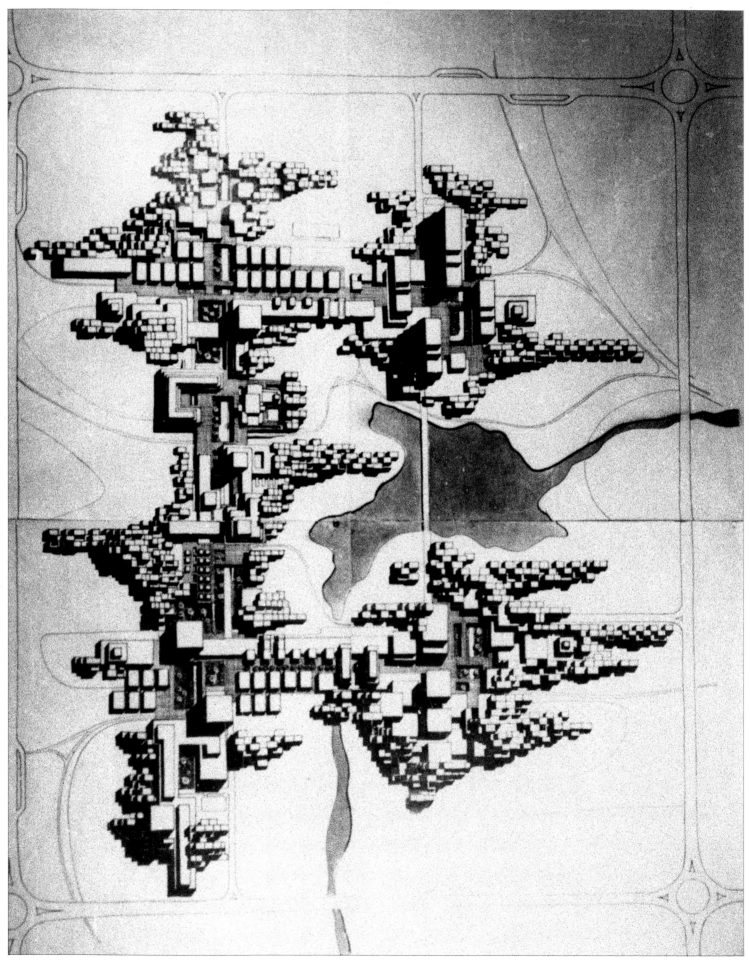

DISTRICT CENTRE, BAGHDAD 1968; *OPPOSITE:* BASIL AL-BAYATI, K AL ANI & T BADIR DISCUSSING THE DESIGN OF PROF GHAZI RESIDENCE, 1967;
COLLEGE OF AGRICULTURE, OMARA 1969; WADIE HOUSE, BASRAH 1969

INTRODUCTION

Basil Al-Bayati was born into a literary family in the old quarter of the City of Baghdad in 1946. Post-War Iraq was in a state of turmoil and social upheaval. It was theoretically an independent state with Britain playing a leading role in its political and economic life. The British were the first to side with the monarchy in shaping what was Mesopotamia into modern Iraq.

The fifties witnessed the resurgence of Arab nationalism which was, and still is, a very strong and powerful political body throughout the Middle East. But this coincided with the resurgence of left-wing politics abroad offering a range of openings from social democracy to communism.

Towards the end of the fifties, the monarchy was toppled by the army and the rule of the officer classes began. There followed a series of coups d'état which created uncertainty and chaos in every aspect of daily life. These developments made schools and universities more involved in politics than in the pursuit of learning. It was a strange and unique era in which not only student theses and research but even building design had political connotations.

Basil Al-Bayati lived and finished his education in this turbulent climate which, in effect, shaped the outlook of his generation. He graduated from Markazia secondary school in the early sixties with a first-class degree and then joined the Department of Architecture within the College of Engineering at Baghdad University. He got a first in Architectural Engineering and became the youngest lecturer at Basra University. After setting up his own practice soon afterwards, he began to compete with established firms of the time. Examples of his work during this period are the Ghazi residence, Baghdad University compound (1968), the Wadie residence, Basra (1969) and the College of Agriculture, Omara (1969).

There were three groups of architects working in Baghdad at that time. The first group, typified by Munir, based their ideas on international modern architecture. The second group, of which Chidirchi is an example, developed a new Iraqi architecture drawing on traditional themes. The third was the Makiya method which adopted traditional features but used new materials and contexts. It was a time of experimentation. The discovery of oil and the subsequent creation of the modern Arab city had transformed the economy of the Gulf area. With rapid development, a new style of architecture, created by Sayid Karim, came to dominate the whole area.

Yet Basil Al-Bayati was dispirited by this approach to architecture. His social views and architectural ideas were considered eccentric in the Arab world and he therefore decided to immerse himself in research and intensive study. He travelled to England to put his ideas into practice in an environment that was not hostile to his work. In the early days he earned a living by undertaking small projects, drawing perspectives of buildings for other architects and ghosting designs for successful architectural practices, while always dreaming of building his own designs.

In the early seventies he was awarded a British Council Scholarship for two years and studied at London University under the supervision of Professor Patrick Wakely. He successfully completed

AL NAKHLAH TELECOMMUNICATION TOWER; *OPPOSITE:* BASIL AL-BAYATI, JAMES QUIBIT, VENICE BIENNALE EXHIBITION, OCTOBER 1982;
WHITE CITY HOTEL & CONFERENCE CENTRE, LONDON 1974; LIVERPOOL STREET STATION REDEVELOPMENT, LONDON 1974

the post-graduate course at the School of Environmental Studies and was awarded the University College Diploma in Development and Planning. It was here that he first made contact with architects from all over the world. After joining the Architectural Association School of Architecture he studied under the supervision of Professor Paul Oliver. On completion of this graduate course he was awarded the AA Graduate Diploma. His research was concerned with the means whereby creativity is assessed. He carried out a year of further research, under the supervision of Andrew Szmidla, on the factors affecting creativity.

In the years that followed he remained a member of the Architectural Association, practising privately as an architect, lecturing and earning his living as a contract architect for a London practice. It was during these years that he made many friends who were also practising architects. One of whom, Ramish Vadgama, introduced him to Leo Grimpel, a partner at Fitzroy Robinson & Partners, who subsequently employed him in his design section. In the mid-seventies, Al-Bayati was involved in the design and presentation of various large projects, including the detailed submission for the White City Stadium site. This development comprised a hotel, an exhibition centre, warehousing and a new greyhound racing stadium. He was also involved in the design of the Liverpool Street/Broad Street redevelopment, comprising a new railway terminal, shops, hotel, civic centre, amenities and offices. This project resulted in his work being held in high regard by all the partners. *The Evening Standard* referred to it as 'a space-age look for Liverpool Street' and *The Guardian* described the scheme as 'a planetarium-look station'.

After a year with Fitzroy Robinson & Partners, Basil Al-Bayati became the Middle-East Consultant. During this period he contributed to the design of various projects in the Middle East. He subsequently joined a number of consortia and, at one stage, headed a design section at Peter Black & Partners.

Basil Al-Bayati has successfully combined the science of engineering with the art of architecture. This interest in structural engineering was furthered by research carried out at the Polytechnic of Central London, under the guidance of Professor Paul Regon. In 1978 the Architects' Registration Council of the United Kingdom directed that his name be entered in the Register of Architects; he was subsequently elected as a corporate member of the Royal Institute of British Architects.

Islamic architecture is a fundamental influence on Al-Bayati's work; derived from his cultural background. His interest was pursued under Professor Geza Fehervari at the University of London where he was awarded, by the Senate, the degree of Doctor of Philosophy.

In the early eighties, Basil Al-Bayati acquired British nationality. He chose to settle in London and to practise architecture there. At that time many people from the Middle East were acquiring properties there and by now Al-Bayati was well known, with many clients beating a path to the door of his Knightsbridge office. He obtained commission after commission and was single-handedly responsible for the restoration of prestigious and sensitive areas of London. Yet the desire to build something with his own characteristic stamp was growing.

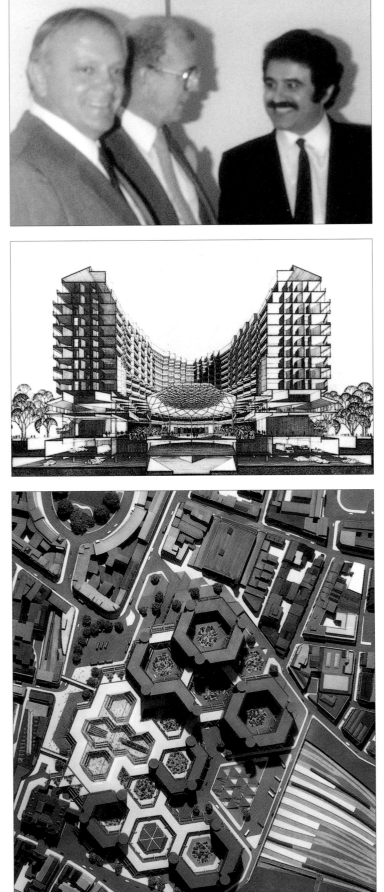

RESIDENTIAL & COMMERCIAL CENTRE, ABU-DHABI; *OPPOSITE:* BASIL AL-BAYATI AND ANNA RICCI DISCUSSING THE HOUSING PROJECT, MARBELLA 1982; COURTYARD HOUSE BASED ON HANGING GARDENS, ELEVATIONS AND SECTIONS

In 1981 Basil Al-Bayati took part in a symposium on the Arab City in Medina, Saudi Arabia. His paper 'Process and Pattern' was subsequently published as a book by AARP with the title *Theory and Practice in Architectural Design for the Arab World*. It offered both new ideas and a fresh approach to design. His paper proved that successful design for the Islamic world rests on an understanding of the cultural elements of the region, embodying the rules handed down by Divine Law. In Islam everything has an outer and an inner meaning; in order to understand anything we have to see both the inner and the outer reality. In his paper he suggested a mechanism for the design process which he called the 'Excitor Apparatus' (Wasitah) which later formed the basis for many of his design projects including Jama'a Al-Kitab and the Al-Nakhlah Telecommunication Tower.

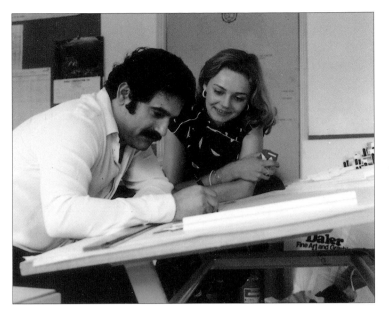

In 1982 Basil Al-Bayati was invited by Paolo Portoghesi, Director of the Architectural Section of the Venice Biennale, to take part in the Second International Exhibition of Modern Islamic Architecture held in Venice, in October of that year. Ten projects were exhibited and particular interest was expressed in the Al-Nakhlah Telecommunication Tower, Jama'a Al-Kitab and the Arabic Guest House. This was the first time that Basil Al-Bayati's work had been exhibited internationally and his reputation now spread beyond Italy to the international community of architects. He took part in many other exhibitions including 'Arab Architecture Past and Present' at the Royal Institute of British Architects and the 'Saudi-British Expo' in Jeddah. Furthermore various architectural magazines began to discuss his work. In 1983 Al Benaa published an article on Chederji, Makiya, Kenzo Tange and Basil Al-Bayati.

The head of the Department of Museums and Antiquities of Saudi Arabia gave Al-Bayati the opportunity to take part in the competition for the Darriyah Cultural Centre at Al-Darriyah, which he won. This project led to several other commissions in Saudi Arabia.

In Kuwait he designed a family residence for Mrs Fatima Al-Essa in Shuwikh, built by Al Hamra Construction. The brief asked for a house with enclosed spaces on different levels, each level representing a separate unit including a guest section, a family section, boys' quarters and girls' quarters. Basil Al-Bayati based his design on the concept of the Hanging Gardens of Babylon which were built by Neguchadnezzar in the sixth century BC for his wife Amytis, the daughter of the King of the Medes. This garden was constructed in a series of ascending tiers so that it resembled a theatre. The structural pattern of the Al-Essa residence, on a square grid basis and rotating in a four-fold pattern at forty-five degrees, is inspired by rotating symmetry. The central part is taken as the origin of growth; it expands a quarter of its size, spreads outwards and then rotates through forty-five degrees.

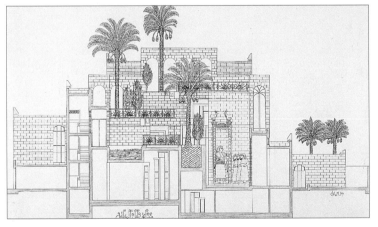

The house became a focal point of Kuwait City. A unique design, it was the first time that palm trees were seen growing on the first, second, third and fourth floors of a building.

The boom in the Gulf gave Basil Al-Bayati a chance to participate in several projects in the United Arab Emirates. The Department of Social Services and the Commercial Building Administration announced a competition to design a commercial and residential complex in Abu-Dhabi. Together with the engineer, Suds Prabhu and others, Basil Al-Bayati formed a consortium, entered the

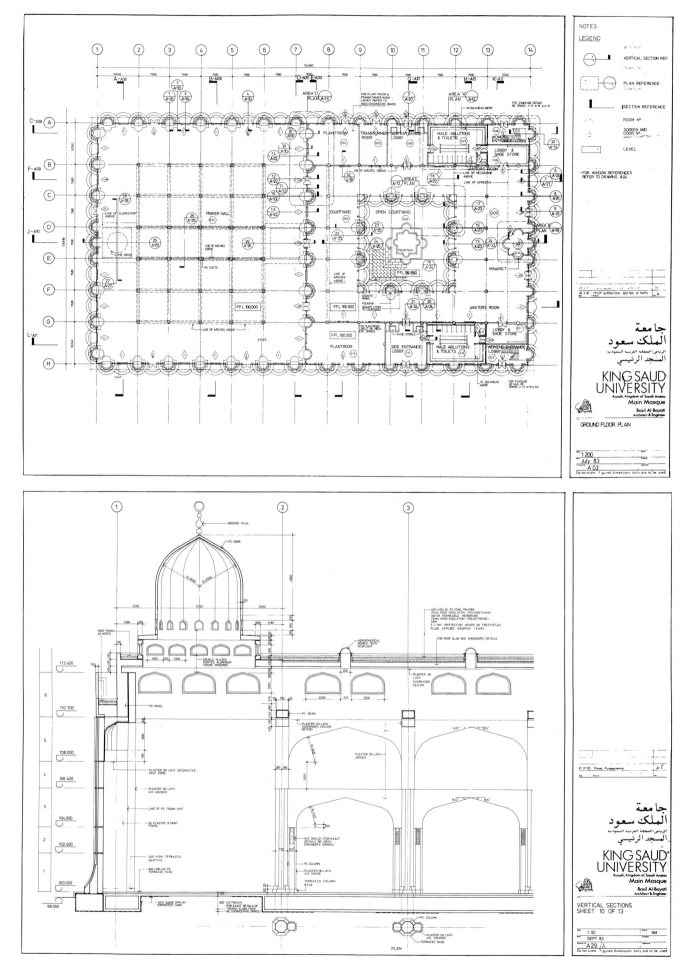

THE PALM MOSQUE, PLAN AND SECTION THROUGH DOME IN FRONT OF MIHRAB; *OPPOSITE:* BASIL AL-BAYATI, STRUCTURAL ENGINEER PETER COX; THE PALM MOSQUE, BIRD'S-EYE VIEW; THE PALM MOSQUE, BUTTRESSES IN THE SHAPE OF PALM TRUNKS; DETAIL OF THE INTERIOR; AXIS TOWARDS THE MIHRAB AREA

competition and came third. It had given Al-Bayati the chance to design a large urban design scheme, the sort of project he preferred.

The design was based on two factors: the courtyard and covered market within the residential and commercial zones which acted as a link to all parts of the community. The architecture of the project concentrates on unity. It is an architecture created by man's concern for Divine Law and how he behaves within this Law in an Islamic Society. In this design Basil Al-Bayati included for the first time the concept of right and wrong in planning.

Right in planning the urban structure of Arab cities should be based on the principle of unity, the whole being made up of cellular units that in turn are made up of smaller segments, each being flexible enough to change in size in order to achieve variety, and each containing a number of elements that can also be used in different ways to give variety to the segment's shape.

The wrong way of planning in an Arab city is to rely on the concept of a detached machine for living where the design of the structure neglects the problem of urban space. After submitting this project, Al-Bayati took the idea further in his book entitled *Community and Unity*, Academy Editions, London, 1983.

In November 1982, the President of King Saud University was looking for a new design scheme for the main mosque of the university. A design, conceived some time before by the university's architect and based on the same architecture as the campus, already existed. The President and the Director-General of the university invited projects from a number of architects, including Basil Al-Bayati who suggested that a building such as a mosque should have its own identity, and not necessarily be read as part of the main complex. Yet this had always been the case in existing mosque designs in urban areas. Al-Bayati asserted that the mosque should have its own scale and proportions and not complement the main buildings. It should have integrity and a sense of purpose. It was his use of symbols which distinguished his design from all others submitted. The elevations contained buttresses in the shape of palm trunks, an historic analogy originating from familiar architectural forms of the past, such as those of the first Islamic community in Medina. The Prophet Mosque was built from palm trunks, a dome in front of the Mihrab derived from early mosques such as Qairawan. The design of the plan was based on a traditional Arab design consisting of a prayer hall and a courtyard. A secular Islamic architecture, comprising buttresses in the shape of palm trunks, revived the old building practices of the Prophet Mosque.

Basil Al-Bayati submitted the proposal to the President of the university and the Director-General of the university project. After examining his proposal and others submitted to them they chose his design. Later he entered into a contract with the university to design the main mosque and to be responsible for all its designs, including architectural and engineering considerations.

The contractors were BBJV, of France and the USA, and their contractor PCG of Stuttgart, Germany. In November 1984 the mosque building appeared in its final form and by January 1985 the mosque was in use for prayer.

Later King Saud University commissioned Basil Al-Bayati to design their entrance gate. He based the design on the concept of faith and knowledge. He ingeniously chose the shape of a book as the

DREAM WORLD: ARABIAN FANTASY AND FANTASY PALACE; *OPPOSITE:* BASIL AL-BAYATI AND FAHIM MAZHARY; KSU ENTRANCE GATE (FAITH AND KNOWLEDGE)

principal element of the design for the university entrance. The books have been placed so that their pages are interlocked, thus representing the close connection between faith and knowledge.

Faith and knowledge in Islam represent parallel paths, for knowledge on its own is not sufficient and will not be totally fulfilled except with faith. Hence faith does not contradict knowledge because religion leads towards knowledge and awareness. Faith is based on acknowledgement of comprehension emerging from knowledge to follow, to behave as it dictates and states; thus to have faith and recognise it as such is the highest degree of wisdom. Islam calls always for faith and knowledge to run in parallel. The book represents one of the lungs with which the human mind breathes.

Various verses in the holy Koran link knowledge and faith together: 'God will lift those faithfuls amongst you and those who have acquired knowledge and climbed many steps and attained higher levels'; 'And these examples we show shall be understood, but only by the knowledgeable people'; 'It is clear verse in the shape of pictures of those who were giving knowledge'.

After the completion of this gateway, Basil Al-Bayati received many other commissions from all over the Middle East. His ability to fuse function and fantasy, and to mould an object physically and psychologically was clearly recognised and admired. In his project, the Dream World, he created a fantasy world inspired by the story *A Thousand and One Tales of the Arabian Nights*. The fantasy palace, the flying house, the magic island and other imaginative designs all fall within a structural pattern based on an original design concept.

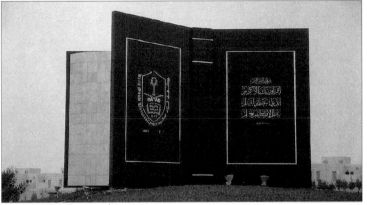

In England in the mid-eighties the property boom gave Al-Bayati the opportunity to design for some exciting schemes such as the Lisson Grove and Hammersmith development and the conversion of the Bliss Tweed Mill in Chipping Norton, where the design of the chimneys influenced the whole design. Chimneys had been the object of his attention from the earliest days, their shape deriving from Islamic minarets and Roman-Italian architecture. His design for the Bliss Tweed Mill was based on the idea of a castle in a park. The mill became the central point of interest extended outwards with buildings, in varying degrees of continuity.

He based the design on a central point of interest which functions as a 'focus', in this instance the mill with its tower. This centre extends with a varying degree of continuity in different directions. In this case, continuity is rhythm, musical rhythm between the whole and the part. Direction is both horizontal and vertical, the direction of earth and sky – the terraces resemble the horizontal and the chimneys resemble the vertical. Centralisation, direction and rhythm are, therefore, the basis of creating this space structure.

He tried to give the complex a special character, just as it had originally. The character of the existing building is derived from particular features, namely the type of windows, doors, curved walls and roofs. These define the barrier between the inside and the outside, and the character of the place is determined by how the building, standing and rising towards the sky, is materialised. The abstract presence of the verticals (chimneys) establishes the general order and gives the first suggestion of the cosmic nature of its character.

Basil Al-Bayati continued his interest in mosques, designing one in Budapest, Hungary. He was given the Gul Baba Turbe site to

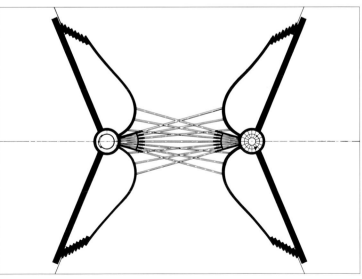

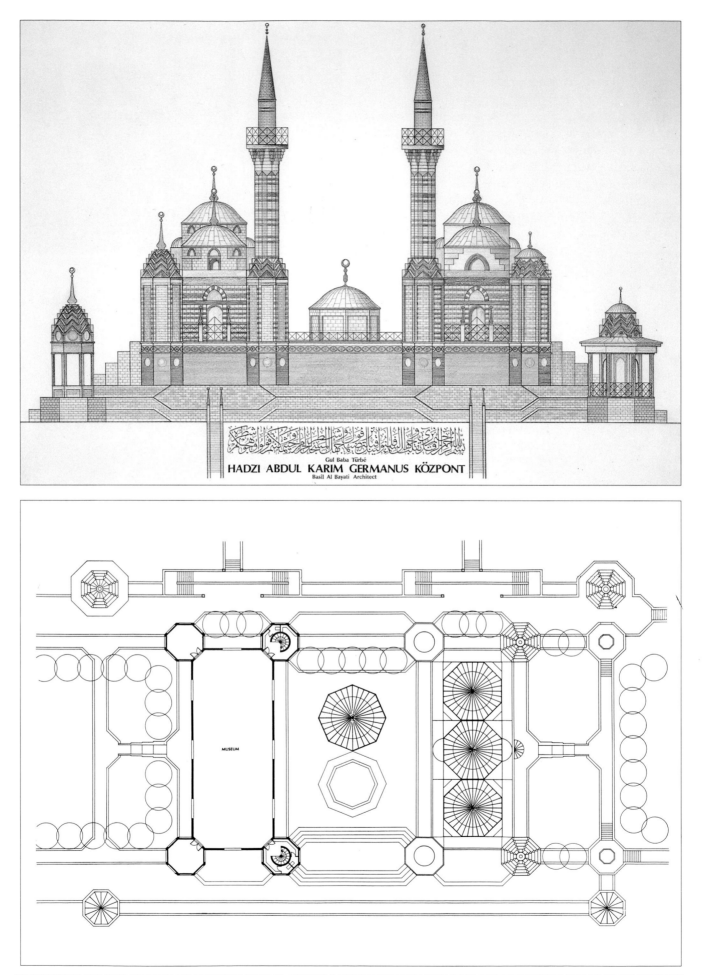

HADZI ABDUL KARIM GERMANUS KÖZPONT
Basil Al Bayati Architect

MUSEUM

ISLAMIC CENTRE, BUDAPEST, HUNGARY, 1987, ELEVATION AND PLAN; *OPPOSITE:* LAYING OF THE FOUNDATION STONE, EDINBURGH MOSQUE: MOHAMMED BIN ASHIQ RIZVI, BASIL AL-BAYATI, ABDUL RAHMAN AL MATROODI; THE GREAT MOSQUE, EDINBURGH, 1987; ISOMETRIC; ELEVATION

house a new Islamic Centre. In England he was commissioned to design mosques for sites in Birmingham, Milton Keynes, Walsall, Leicester and Edinburgh.

In Edinburgh the principal functions have influenced the form. The sanctuary comprises seven perpendicular aisles, two are parallel to the Gibla. The location of the dominant naves is reminiscent of the 'T' plan, while the two domes at the extremities of the central nave recall the early North-African mosques. The local building traditions, art and symbols are used in such a way as to result in the creation of a specifically local type of mosque architecture; for example the Scottish castle plays a part in the design. Abstract patterns from vernacular art merge with Kufic calligraphy to become an integral part of the decorative element. The tartan and check-like arrangement of the tartan patterns are a symbol of clan kinship in Scotland.

The other dominant feature of the Great Mosque in Edinburgh is the creation of a courtyard through the positioning of the building mass. The size and shape of the courtyard has been manipulated to maximum effect, in recognition of its importance as the first step in getting into the mosque area. However, it is important to emphasise that the climate of Scotland is much harsher than that in most of the Islamic world. As a result, the courtyard could not be utilised in the same way, although it still functions as an important intermediate space. Traditionally, the mosque position within the urban structure appeared in two forms. In the first, the mosque was faced on four sides by Ziadas and the palace usually adjoined the qibla wall. In the case of the Great Mosque of Edinburgh, because of the shape of the site, the location of the building mass is arranged in such a way that the mosque appears as a free-form praying area, which leads off to the study area or Madrasa. It is important to emphasise such an arrangement, as historically the advent of Islam brought with it inevitable architectural change to established and flourishing cities. The Moslem population restricted their political and social activities to within the confines of the mosques, which functioned as meeting places. Thus street squares gradually disappeared, to be replaced by courtyards. In the case of the Pottersow site, three spaces have been created within the urban structure. The first is the sanctuary or holy space; the second space is the street, or unholy space; while the third is the courtyard which acts as a transitional space between the holy and unholy spaces.

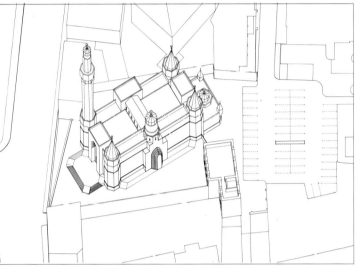

The line of division between courtyard and sanctuary has been carefully selected as guiding to the 'right path' and involves going through an entrance area which is higher up. A dome recessed in the ceiling signifies the dividing line between the holy and unholy.

Mowlem (Scotland) was awarded the building contract and in 1987 the foundation stone of the Great Mosque in Edinburgh was laid.

During the eighties many post-modern architects became interested in designing furniture, resulting in prolific furniture and interior design throughout this period. On his frequent trips to Italy, Basil Al-Bayati acquired many contacts in the business of manufacturing furniture; and it was the Pologna family of Cantu who made most of his designs during this period. Stalactite capitals, based on the three-lobed squinch of tenth-century Asia, were used in the design of the column suite. Palm trees, the essential element in Islamic architecture, were introduced in the design of the palm suite,

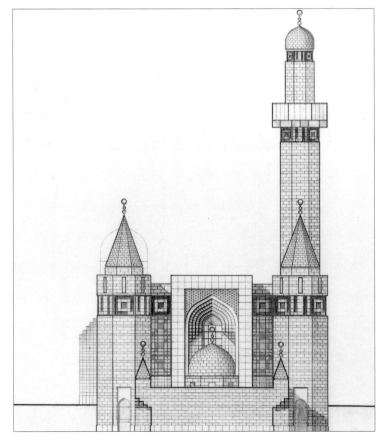

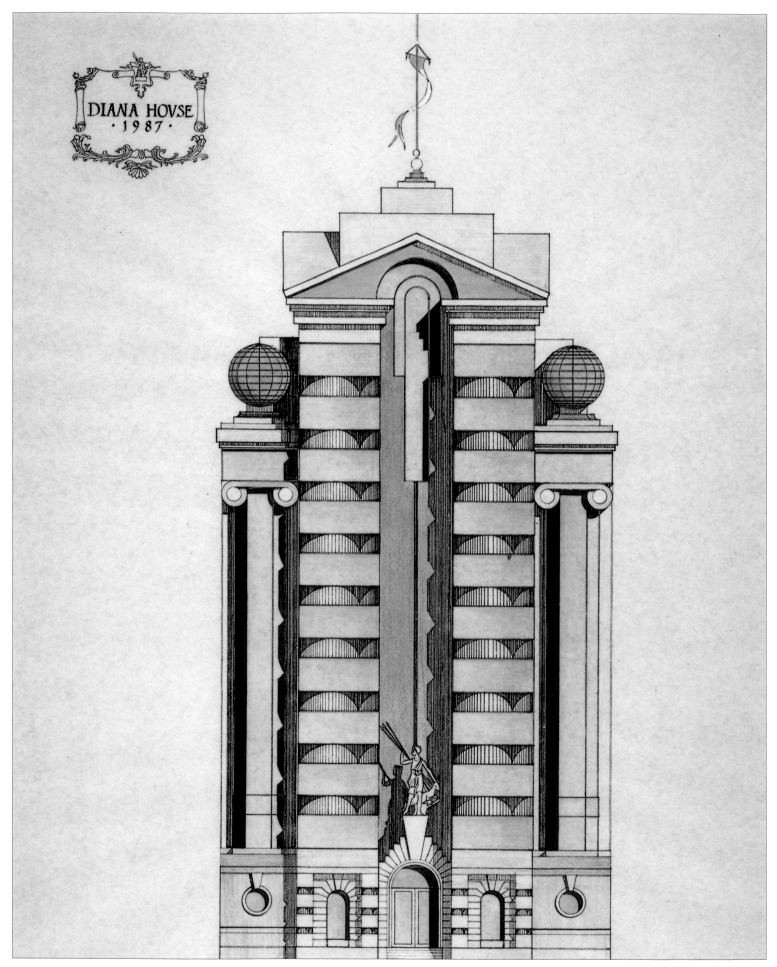

DIANA HOUSE, LISSON GROVE, LONDON; *OPPOSITE:* THE JURY: ARAB TOWN ORGANISATION AWARDS, DOHA, 1989, BASIL AL-BAYATI, ABDUL LATEEF AL-HIJJAMI, ABDUL BAQI IBRAHIM, TALIB AL-TALIB, IBRAHIM CHBBOUH, SALEH AL-HATHLOUL; HAMMERSMITH ROAD, LONDON; CHURCH ISLAND HOUSE, RIVERSIDE ELEVATION

while the shape of the Persian tomb towers with fluted walls were the focus elements in the tower suite.

In the late eighties, Basil Al Bayati obtained many prestigious commissions in England, Europe and the Middle East from many influential clients. One such commission was to conceive a new residence, in the English turn-of-the-century manner, on an island in the Thames. His design evokes the English Arts and Crafts movement, notably Lutyens' vernacular houses and projects by Baillie Scott and Voysey. The internal volumes are identified by the juxtaposition and intersection of two tiers of four equal spaces and these are supplemented with a row of three equally-sized spaces on the ground floor, establishing a three-dimensional grid where the access of the L-shaped formation intersects the meeting plane of the space below. The vertical faces of these spaces are punctuated by projections and recesses, some of decreasing size, in the form of chimneys, windows and alcoves.

Bedrooms and bathrooms are on two levels within a double volume space. The upper level overlooks the living quarters via an open balustrade, while the recreation area occupies the short wing, rising into double height and is visually linked to the living area through a glazed screen. The three aligned spaces on the ground floor contain a kitchen, a dining area and services.

The main axis of the building runs east to west, parallel to the south bank, from which the terrace overhangs. The building is approached from the east side, via a pathway which also provides access to the ferry. The veranda to the west commands a long view over the Thames and is focused on a gazebo strategically placed at the far end of the island. A miniature lock will be cut into the island for boat maintenance and repairs. The vertical features – chimneys and brick bays extended above roof level – emerge from the ground or are cantilevered from the wall. The main roof and full-height windows express the internal spaces and hold all the elements of architectural composition together as a coherent whole.

Following this project Basil Al-Bayati obtained other commissions for the design of country houses in Middlesex and Windsor, as well as Kensington and Chelsea in Central London. He has presided over panels and juries such as the jury for the Arab Towns Organisation which awards a prize every two years, namely the Arab Town Organisation Award in Architecture, Heritage and Engineering. In England and the Middle East he is an adviser to the editorial board of architectural magazines. An active participant in international competitions, he was recently awarded third prize in the Las Terrenas competition by the Canadian developer Las Terrenas Investments Incorporated. Other recent projects include a brief to devise a corporate image for an influential property company, on the basis of his architectural philosophy.

Basil Al-Bayati's work is easily recognisable for its distinctive style and his approach to the living environment will leave a mark on the history of architecture in recent times. This is testified by his continual exposure in many international exhibitions, most recently at the Museum of Art in Frankfurt, Germany.

He will be acknowledged for his humanity and his quest for a profound meaning in his designs, where symbolism and function become one entity.

Editorial

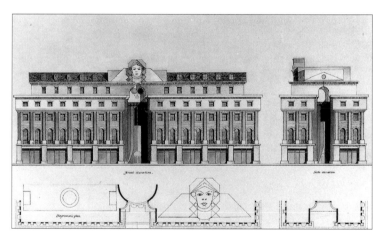

Church Island House.

PROJECTS 1988 - 1992

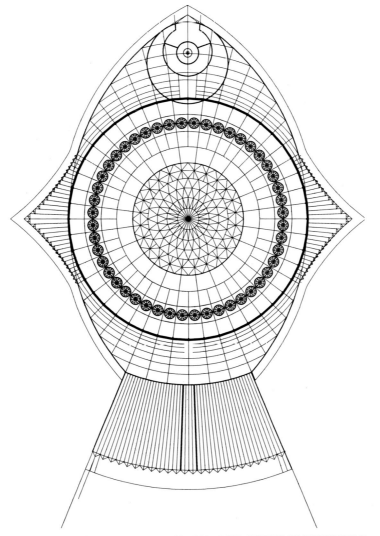

OPPOSITE: COLLEGE FOR ISLAMIC STUDIES, OXFORD; *ABOVE:* SHOPPING COMPLEX IN SOHAIR

MORNING FLOWER RESIDENCE
WARDAT AL-SABAH, 1988

Warda't Al – Sabah
Basil Al–Bayati Architect

GROUND FLOOR PLAN AND SECTION, 1988

Warda't Al – Sabah
Basil Al–Bayati Architect

SITE PLAN AND ELEVATION, 1988

THE OLD BOAT HOUSE

CHURCH ISLAND, 1988

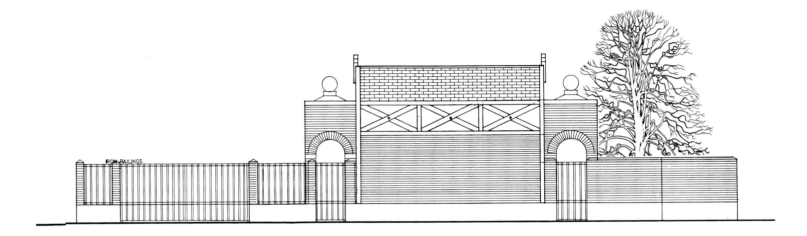

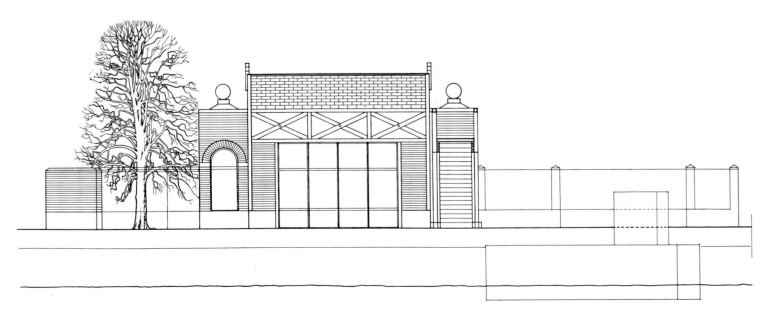

CHURCH STREET AND RIVER SIDE ELEVATIONS

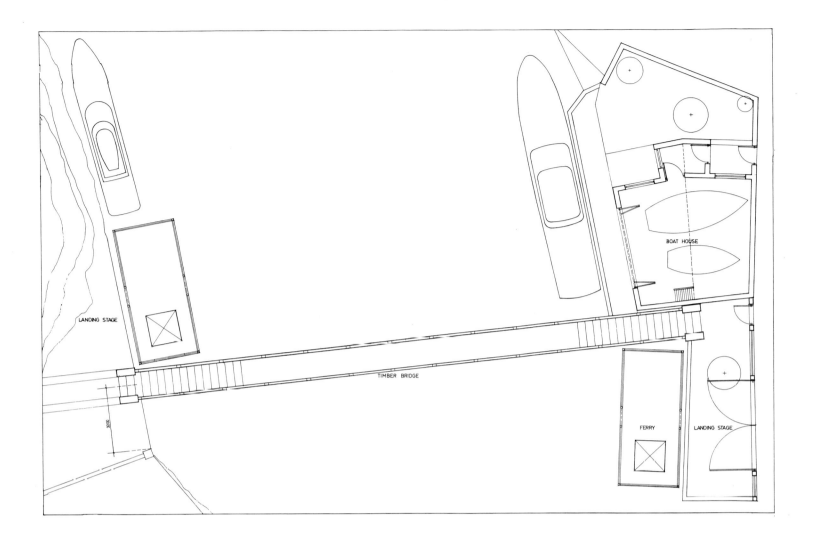

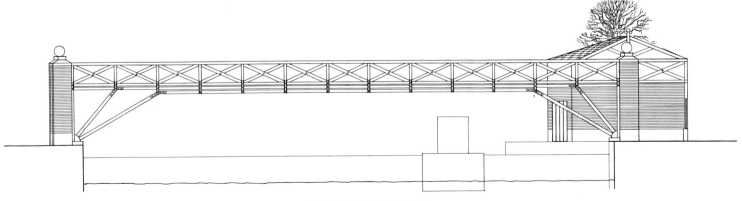

PLAN AND BRIDGE ELEVATION

HOUSE IN RIYADH, 1988

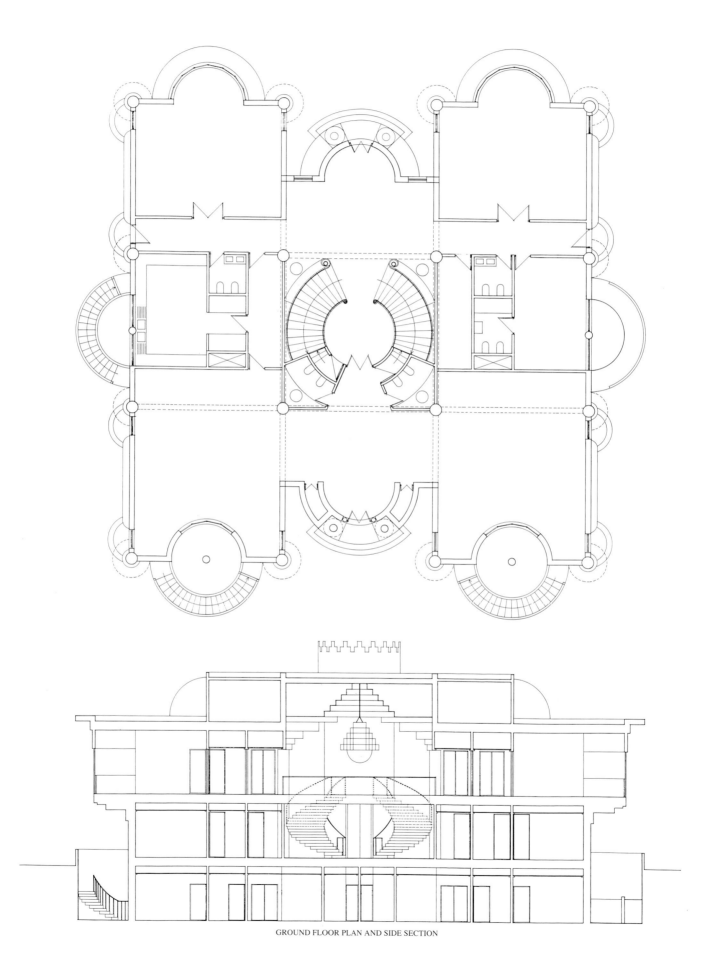

GROUND FLOOR PLAN AND SIDE SECTION

28

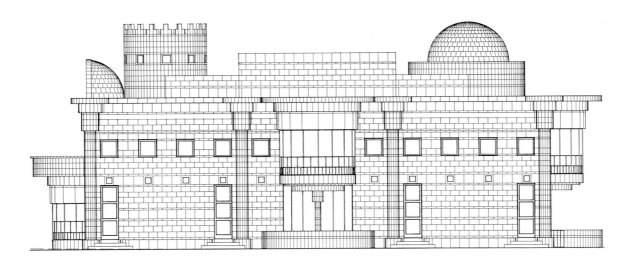

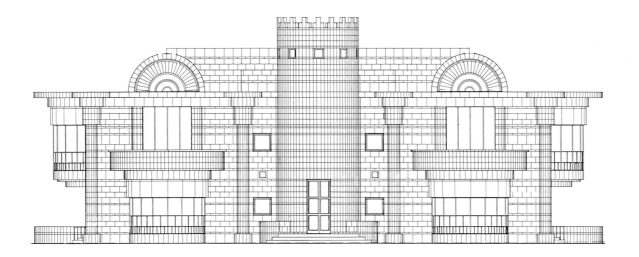

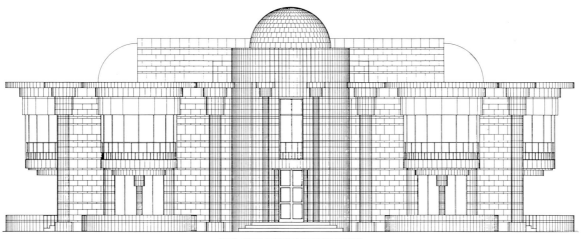

SIDE, REAR AND FRONT ELEVATIONS

ORIENTAL VILLAGE BY THE SEA
DOMINICAN REPUBLIC, 1988

The Oriental Village by the Sea project rules stipulated that provision must be made for a hotel, condominiums, villas and sports facilities. This was interpreted using modern technology to create daring and dramatic structures with individuality and impact being the main goals. The concept of the design was based on the history and culture of the Orient but the plan itself was built around two major elements: the animal and the plant kingdoms.

The ecoskeleton of the animal provides the nucleus of the plan. At the front, the head of the animal forms a circle, with the tail at the opposite end, providing sufficient space for two open amphitheatres.

The second element component, as stated above, is the plant kingdom. The main causeway is in the shape of the branch of a tree. From this, several smaller roads branch off forming leaf-shaped areas; these are the condominiums. At the top of the main tree branch are flower-shaped areas; it is here that the villas will be located.

Examining the plan in detail, starting from the head of the animal, which is situated on the seafront, the onlooker is confronted with the first major structure. The facade of this building, which is in fact the entrance and reception area of the hotel, is in the shape of a large Central Asian nomad tent, a *yurt*.

It is a steel-domed building with two entrances, one to the left and the other to the right. These represent the eyes of the animal. Between these are the steps which are in turn separated by stepped waterfalls reminiscent of the waterfalls of the Mughal gardens of India.

At the top of the steps is a series of arched openings representing the teeth of the animal. Steel was used in the roof to give an impression of space and light. A number of tall skylights in the shape of Japanese fans are located on the roof of the building. The glass in these skylights will be suitably decorated and painted.

On entering the building, the onlooker finds himself in a large domed area which has several mezzanine floors. The centre of the highest dome is open to the sky, enabling the stars to be clearly visible from the interior. This idea was borrowed from Sasanian palace architecture, and at the time it was a symbol of royalty.

The body of the animal provides the space for the hotel rooms, which are arranged on three floors. The facade of these rooms is formed by a series of arches with semicircular arches on the top floor and the upper parts of the windows are shaped like stalactites, or the *mugarnas* of Islamic architecture. The overall impression, however, is that of the Sasanian royal palaces. The rooms can be joined together to form one, two or three bedroom flats ensuring flexibility within a fixed framework.

The corridor which runs the length of the hotel, from the head of the animal to its tail, ie, to the two amphitheatres, represents the animal's spine. The ceiling is formed by a series of small domes, each with an opening to the sky, recalling the covered souks of the Near East. Again, these domes represent royalty and reflect the entrance and reception areas.

There are atriums on all three floors which break up the space and create a more human environment. These atriums incorporate, among other things, waterfalls and palm trees and are specifically designed to encourage people to visit the area. There is a delicate balance between too much and too little space and these atriums are designed to produce a compromise between the two. The overall effect is that of a town within a town, the complex providing everything the onlooker could wish for: shops, coffee shops, restaurants and discotheques.

When the onlooker arrives at the tail of the animal, or at the end of the corridor, he is able to see a series of tall, joined arches. These give the impression of a Chinese pagoda, from inside and out. The arches gradually decrease as one approaches the end of the building, ensuring a feeling of continuity. On leaving the building, the onlooker is confronted with the seats of the two amphitheatres which are formed in two semi-circles. Behind these rows there are small domed kiosks; these represent the *chatris* of Mughal architecture. The combination of the two styles creates a conflict and a tension which lends itself to the dramatic atmosphere necessary for such a structure.

The main causeway is designed in the style of Chinese gardens and is flanked by trees and flowers. To the left a covered walkway branches off into an area which is in the shape of three leaves. Two of these provide space for the condominiums while the third, which is in the shape of a palm tree, is the swimming pool. The covered walkways are designed to imitate Chinese architecture, in particular resembling temples with their characteristic brackets and gables.

The buildings of the two condominiums, with their tall gable roofs, recall the shape of South-East Asian pagodas or meeting halls. The side elevations of the condominiums have the appearance of leaves ending in small dragon figures. It is a simple but effective form, making it unmistakably Oriental. Shape, space and light are all taken into consideration and in some respects the two latter elements are of highter import. On this basis, a skylight has been built into the centre of the leaf in the communal parts of the condominiums allowing light to filter in from outside, casting many fleeting shadows and lending character to this area. Everything in the common area is symmetrical, one side reflecting the other and the entire area can be seen all at once. The basis of the planning of the condominiums is that man should be surrounded by sufficient light and space to provide a tranquil atmosphere.

Amongst the leaves are small circular glass kiosks with merlon-domes resembling the dome of Timur's resting place, the Gur-i Mir in Samarkand. The same type of arrangement is repeated further to the right, where a walkway branches off again into the second group of condominiums. Here we find three leaves and two palmettes. Two of the leaves are condominiums and the palmettes are the swimming pools. The third leaf is a sports centre. The four small circles which are situated between the two condominiums are palm trees.

The main causeway ends between the tail of the animal and the condominium just described. Walkways of varying lengths branch off from here giving access to the villas. These villas are all cylindrical and one or two storeys high with a tall conical roof; recalling Chinese prayer halls or circular temples. The roof tiles of the walkways will be an unobtrusive green resembling the greenery found in the natural world.

The plan has been designed with the human aspect very much in mind. Different permutations of light, space, materials and structure lend themselves to an atmosphere that provides variety as opposed to monotony, while still retaining an air of continuity. The surroundings are also pleasing to those living within the complex. Furthermore the whole structure and design is one of a functional complex. It is fictional architecture, Oriental architecture interpreted in the modern way.

Basil Al-Bayati

Key for the following pages:

1a	Car entrance to village	15	Hotel rooms on 3 floors	b	Lobby and commercial area: 1st floor	b	2-bedroom hotel condominiums
b	Car exit from village	16	Main car access to village			c	3-bedroom hotel condominiums
2a	Car entrance to hotel	17	Covered pedestrian path	c	Rooms: 2nd floor		
b	Car exit from hotel	18	Pedestrian waiting area	d	De luxe suite: top floor	32	Villas
3	Car waiting area	19	Atrium	24	Rooms on all floors	a	1 bedroom, 1 living room, kitchen, bathroom
4	Car park: ground floor	20a	Service area: ground floor	25	Palm tree		
5	Fountain and waterfall	b	Commercial rental area: 1st floor	26	Condominium unit:	b	2 bedrooms, 1 living room, kitchen, bathroom
6	Waiting area			a	1-bedroom condominiums		
7	Hall: 1st floor, Boathouse: ground floor	c	Restaurant and bar: 2nd floor	b	2-bedroom condominiums	c	3 bedrooms, 1 living room, kitchen, bathroom
		d	Discotheque: top floor	c	3 bedroom condominiums		
8	Vertical circulation core	21a	Service area: ground floor	27	Swimming pool	33	Open air parking
9	Sitting area	b	Commercial rental area: 1st floor	28	Conservatory area	34	Open air amphitheatre, car park underneath
10	Bar with mezzanine floor			29	Gym and sauna		
11	Coffee lounge with mezzanine floor	c	Kitchen: 1st floor	30	Service area	35	Special VIP boxes for amphitheatre
		d	Bar: top floor	31	Hotel condominium:		
12	Administration area	22	Presidential suite on 3 floors	a	1-bedroom hotel condominiums	36	Community centre: ground floor
13	Concierge	23a	Service area: ground floor				
14	Service room						

AXONOMETRIC

PERSPECTIVES

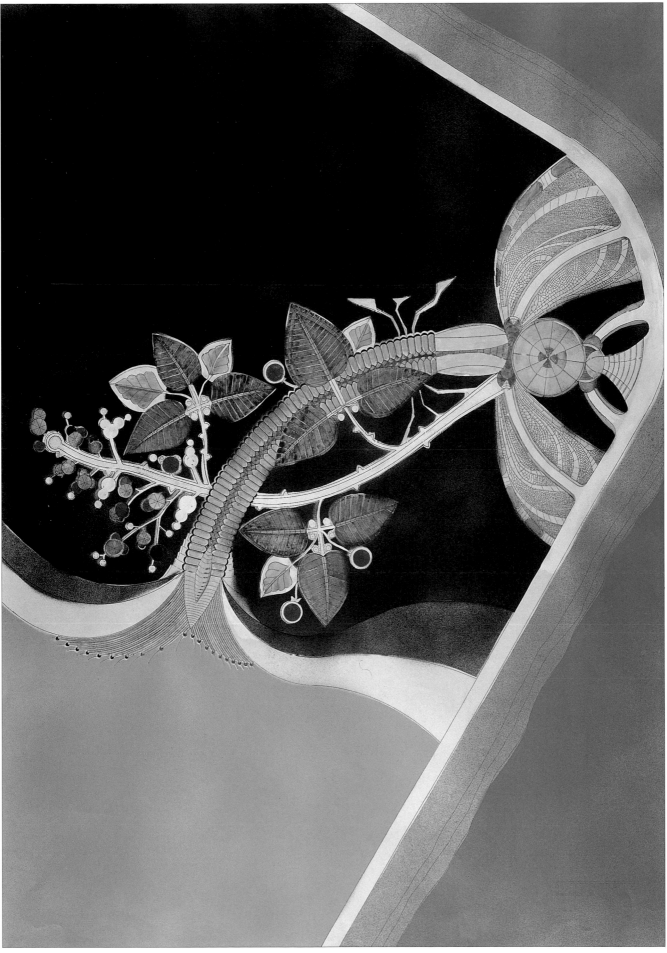

PLAN

PLAN AND ELEVATION OF MAIN HOTEL

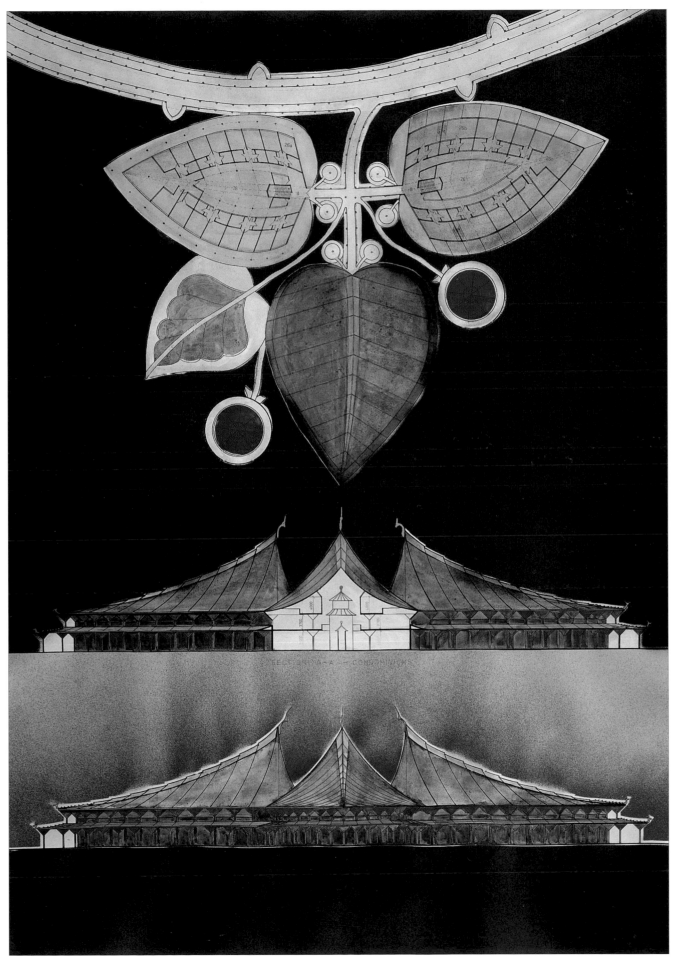

PLAN, SECTION AND ELEVATION OF CONDOMINIUM BLOCK

PLAN AND ELEVATION OF THE AMPHITHEATRE

PLAN, SECTION AND ELEVATION OF RESIDENTIAL UNITS

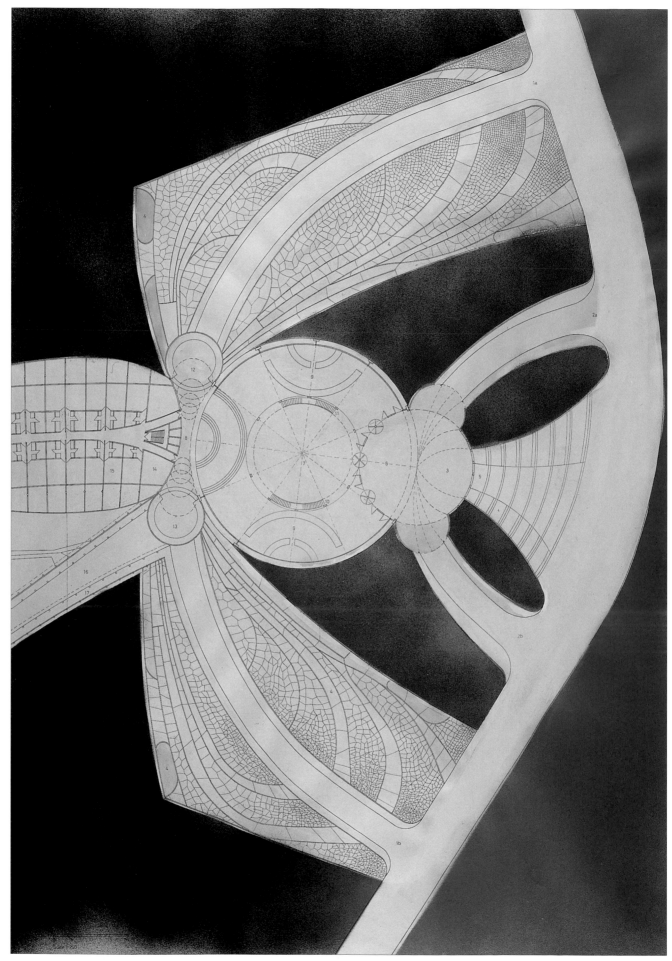

PARTIAL PLAN OF THE HOTEL

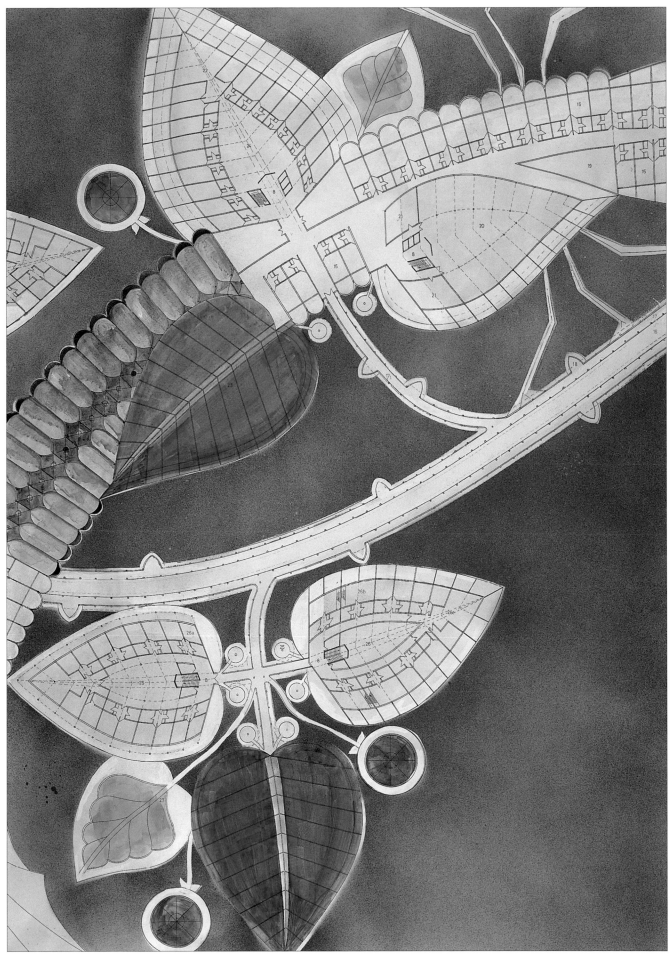

PARTIAL PLAN OF CONDOMINIUMS AND HOTEL

PARTIAL PLAN OF CONDOMINIUMS, RESIDENTIAL UNITS AND AMPHITHEATRE

GENERAL PLAN

LORD'S VIEW II, LONDON
PENTHOUSE & DUPLEXES, 1989

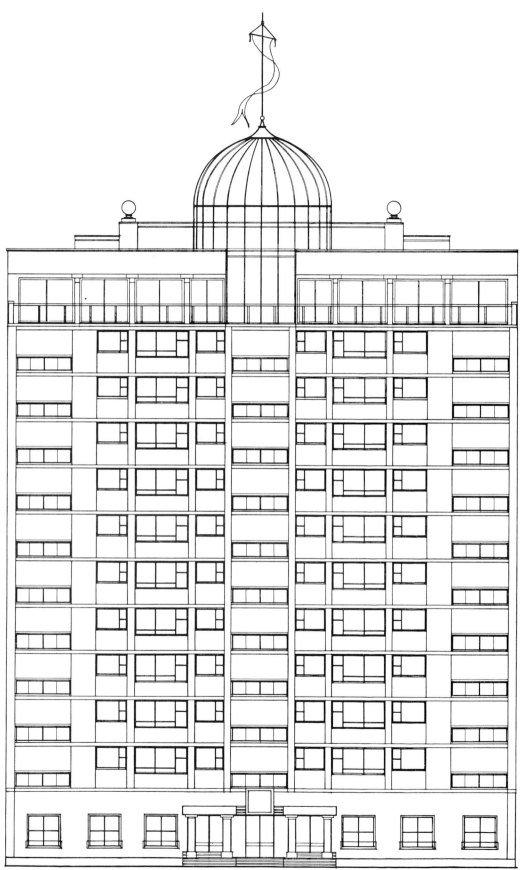

ELEVATION TO ST JOHN'S WOOD ROAD

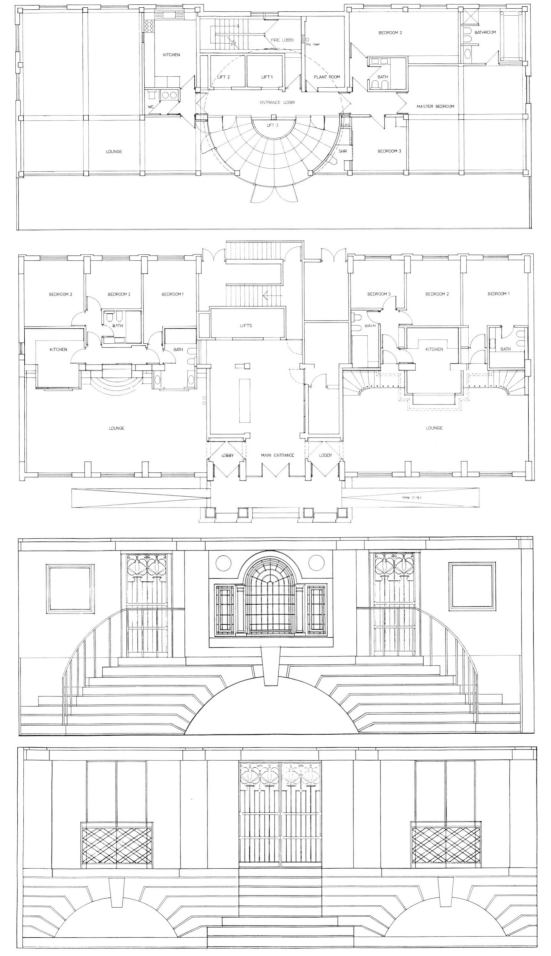

THE PENTHOUSE AND GROUND FLOOR PLANS; ELEVATIONS OF MAIN WALL

PRESIDENTIAL PALACE

SANA'A, 1989

PARTIAL ELEVATIONS OF EASTERN GATE, WESTERN GATE AND OF THE MAIN ARCADE

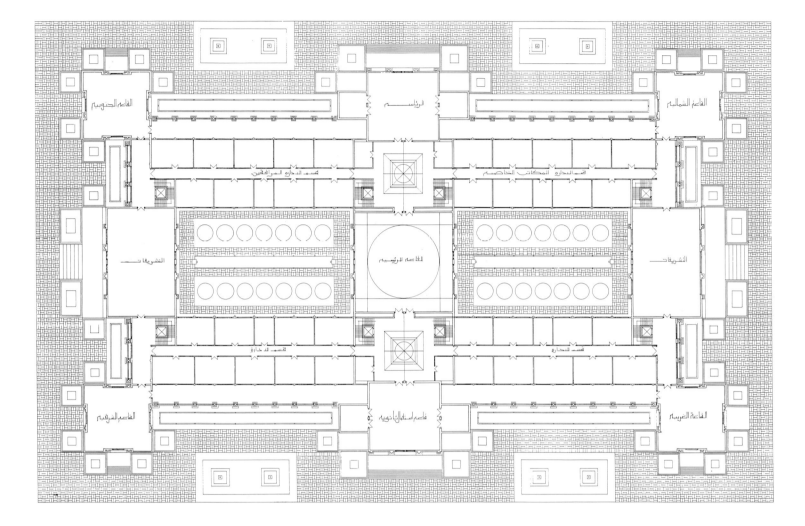

PLAN AND BACK ELEVATION

SIDE ELEVATION OF PALACE

FRONT ELEVATION OF PALACE

BIBLIOTHECA ALEXANDRIA
ALEXANDRIA, EGYPT, 1989

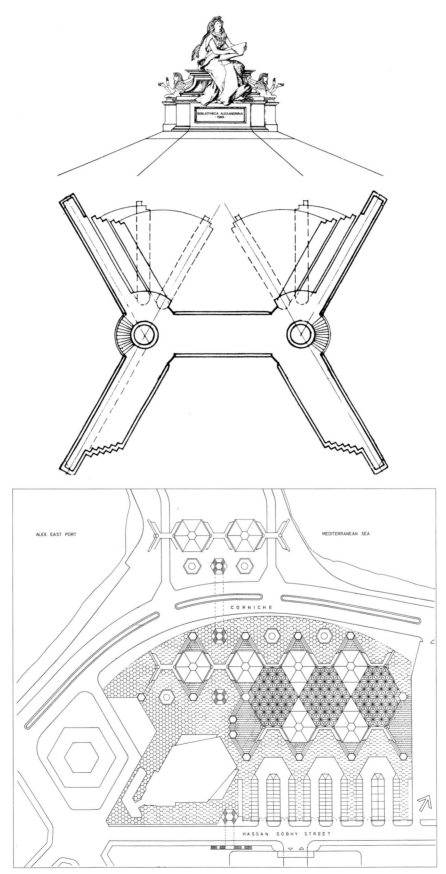

DETAILS OF STATUE OVER ENTRANCE GATE AND OF SEGMENT; SITE PLAN

PERSPECTIVES AND PARTIAL PLANS

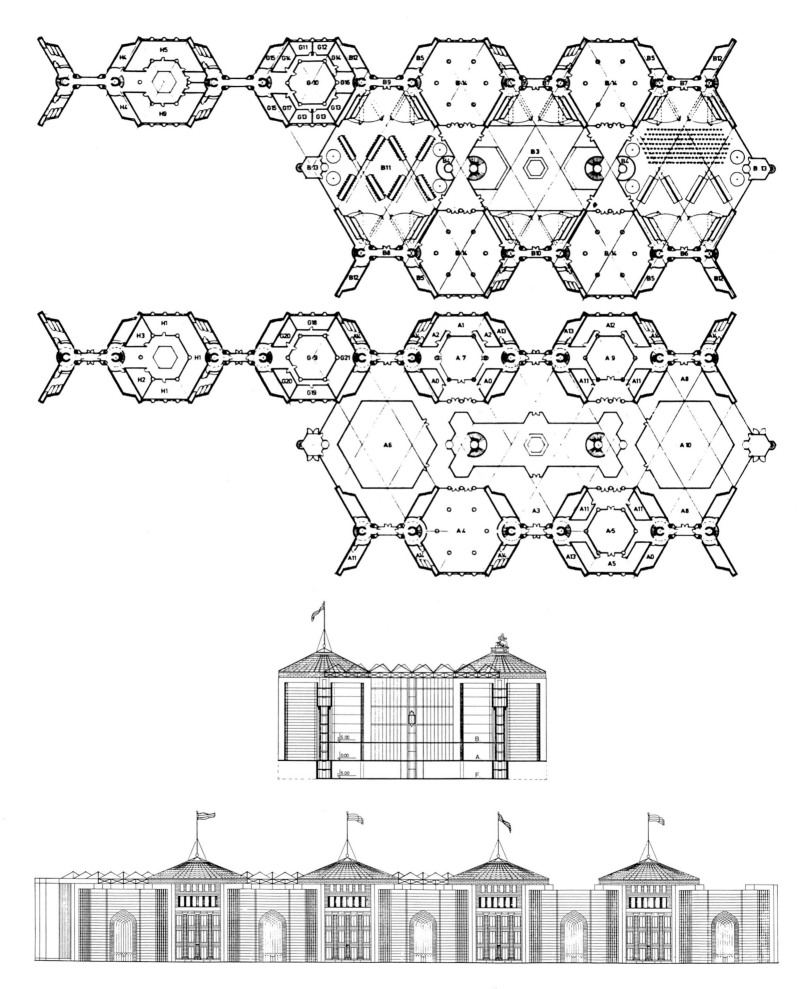

FIRST AND GROUND FLOOR PLANS; SECTION AND ELEVATION

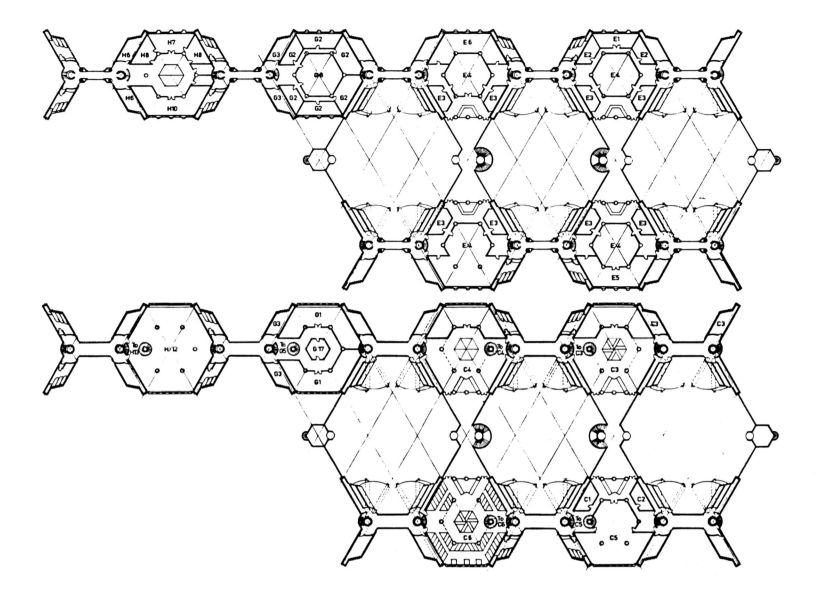

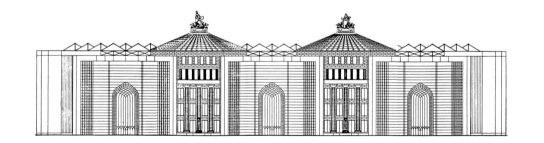

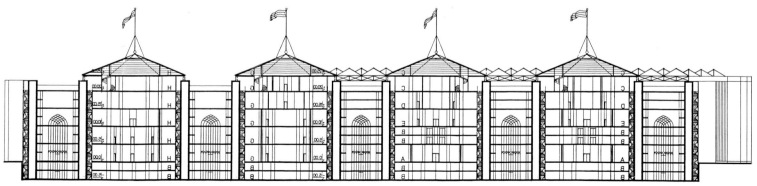

SECOND AND FOURTH FLOOR PLANS; ELEVATION AND SECTION

COMMERCIAL & RESIDENTIAL BUILDING

SANA'A, ZUBARY STREET, YEMEN, 1989

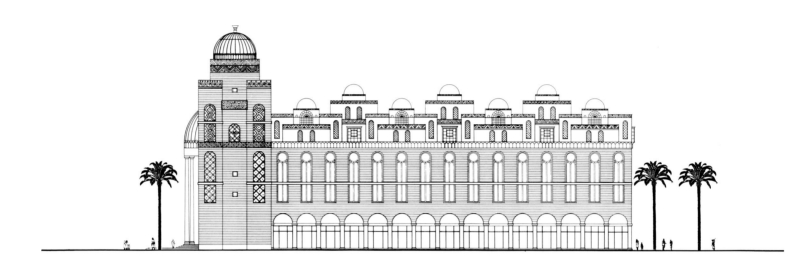

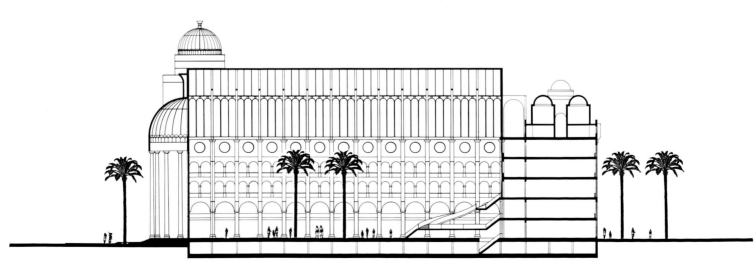

SIDE ELEVATION AND LONGITUDINAL SECTION THROUGH ATRIUM

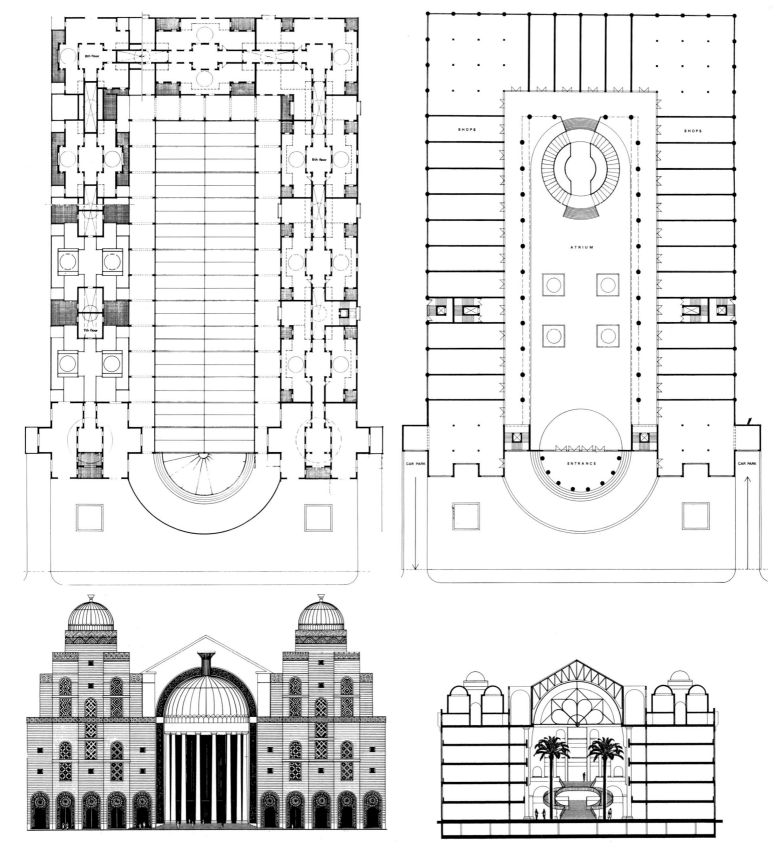

FIFTH, SIXTH AND SEVENTH FLOORS; GROUND, FIRST FLOOR SHOPS, SECOND, THIRD AND FOURTH FLOOR OFFICES;
FRONT ELEVATION FROM ZUBARY STREET; CROSS SECTION THROUGH ATRIUM

MEDINA QABOOS SCHOOL

MUSCAT, OMAN, 1990

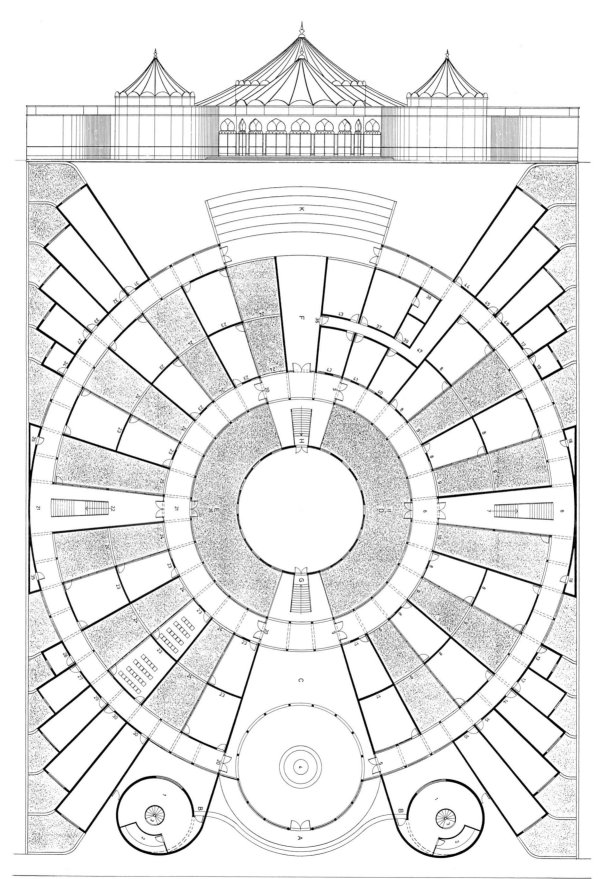

ELEVATION AND GROUND FLOOR PLAN

HYDE PARK
KENSINGTON, LONDON, 1990

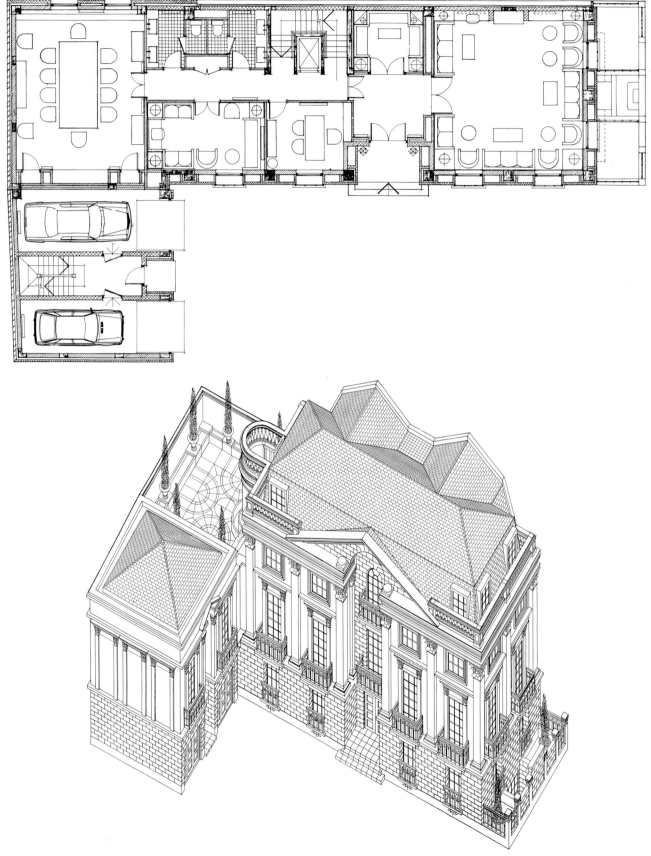

GROUND FLOOR PLAN AND AXONOMETRIC

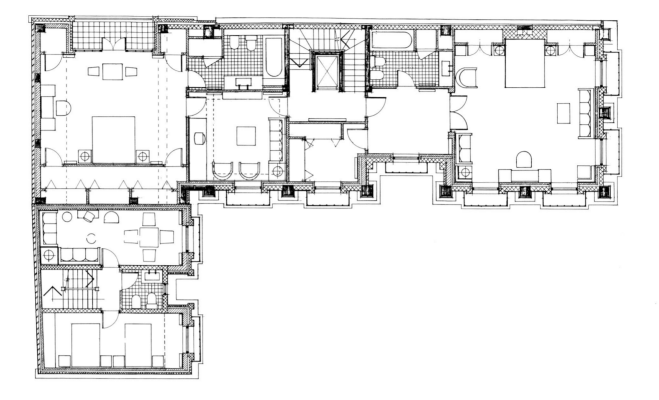

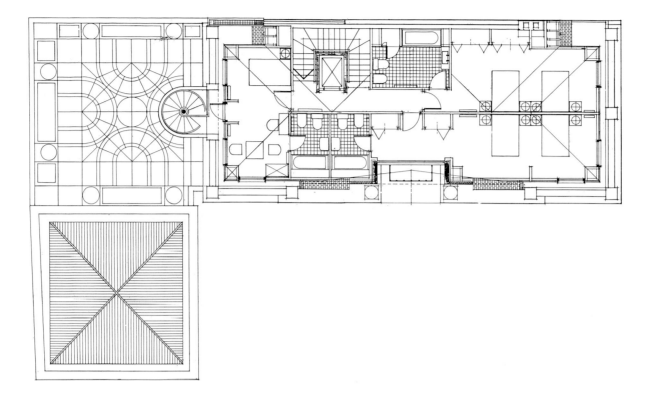

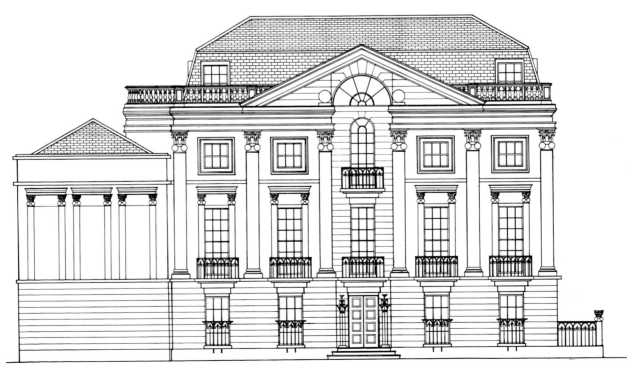

OPPOSITE: FIRST FLOOR PLAN; SECTION; ELEVATION; *ABOVE:* THIRD FLOOR PLAN; ELEVATION

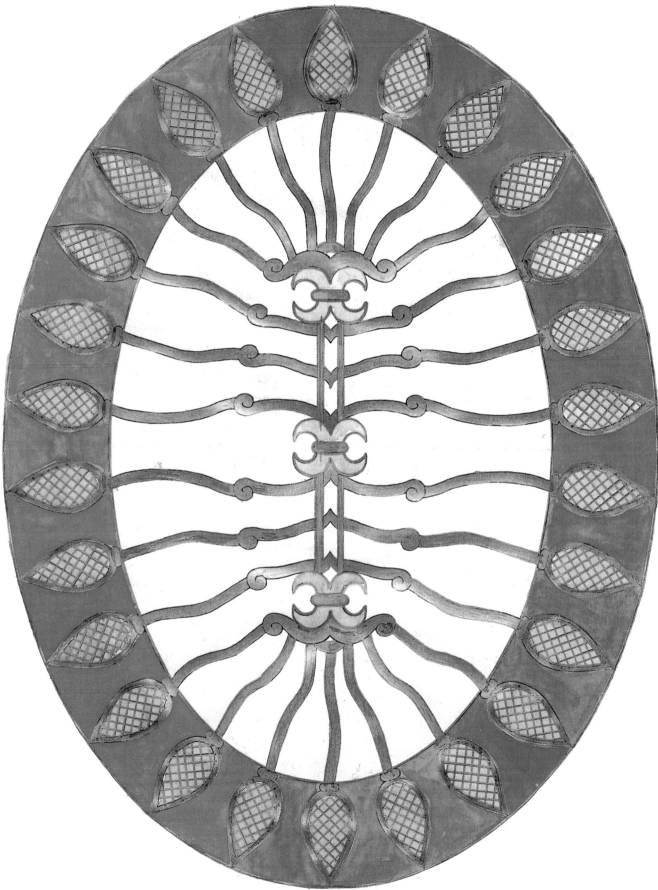

OVAL DISH

BASE TRAY AND PLATE

OVAL DISH

PLATE, CUTLERY AND CUP

SINMAR PALACES, 1990

The complex contains many buildings, each fulfilling one or more functions. The site has been divided into two zones: the public and the private zone. The design of the Sinmar Palaces Compound involved the consideration of many aspects and criteria. The design had to be not only functional and practical but also convey a sense of authority and prestige appropriate to the owner's rank. This is achieved by the principle of unity which results from the successful combination and blend of the various elements constituting its interesting architectural style.

The architecture of the villas is the architect's interpretation of the owner's brief. The circular shape adopted as the planning principle has the added dimension of being the geometry associated with the habitation of divinity, and in addition it is combined in this enchanted environment with the fascination of nature.

The building is located in such a way that it appears to be part of the landscape. It is situated in an enclosed garden with high walls, rose gardens, fruit trees, green bushes, palm trees, flowerbeds, numerous herbs and lawns with borders of entwined hedges. Pergolas and fountains appear in extraordinary settings among the various architectural components.

The setting is theatrical. There are many novelties in every aspect of the design, but uniform characteristics occur throughout the project. The planning of the complex is based on the human body: the central part corresponds to the torso and the axis of symmetry to the spine. The various units are the expression of a great and complex movement.

The design translates ancient and modern aspirations and ideas into urban and architectonic terms.

The Entrance

This is an impressive gateway. It is comprised of three buildings each with its own gateway, including divided driveways for each zone. The central gateway consists of an arch surmounted by a row of classical columns. Additional columns run along the entire length of the entrance.

Main Reception and Banqueting Hall

This building is located in the area between the two zones so that it can be used for both public and private receptions. It has easy access to the main kitchen. An entrance hall has been incorporated in which to receive and greet guests before they proceed to the saloon. The entrance contains two doors: one from the public section, the other from the private section.

The building is sometimes used by the public only, and at other times by women only. The entrance opens onto a monumental staircase which leads to the two upper floors.

The architecture of the building is absolutely symmetrical. The facade consists of an entirely circular central section, flanked in turn by two massive towers whose shape contrasts well with the central form. The facade is divided into sections. On the ground floor the building incorporates some of the elements of a bridge with its peaks and columns, so that the river runs in an imaginary setting. On the first floor the reception room is to the left and the dining hall to the right. On the second floor there is an unbroken series of columns which creates a charming play of light and shadow.

Recreation Building for Private Use and Annexe for Servants

On the other side of the Al Nakheel garden there is a building which has similar characteristics to the main reception and banqueting hall, except that it has a very large hole in the middle which contains the swimming pool. This building is the recreation centre for the family. In addition to the central swimming pool there are two smaller pools on either side of this main pool.

The ground floor contains the changing rooms, massage and beauty rooms, snack bar, sauna and jacuzzi.

The main hall also has two spiral staircases leading to a gallery on the first floor. The facade of this building, like the banqueting hall, is symmetrical with towers on either side. It can be approached through an entrance hall from two sides. The two towers lead to two terraces on either side of the building, these lead in turn to two sections containing an annexe for servants, with their bedrooms, dining rooms and reception rooms adjacent.

The axis leading between the main reception and banqueting hall building (B), and the family recreation building (C), links directly to the villa compound.

The Main Villa

The main villa is situated on the top of a hill. It is a pleasant place which overlooks the surrounding area yet is secluded and hidden from view behind the garden walls. The villa nestles on top of the hill which recedes gradually downwards in the form of a hanging garden. The villa has a circular roof garden called the Moon Garden (Hadikat Al Qamar). This garden crowns the villa, just as the villa crowns the hilltop hanging garden. The building elements are almost an extension of the landscape.

The main villa is grandiose, especially when one views the section spanned by six columns with pediments at the centre and two wings on the sides.

The main villa entrance is on the opposite side facing the terrace garden. The entrance then leads to the spacious central room on the ground floor called the Peacock Hall. Its walls are adorned with friezes of mythological scenes from the story of *A Thousand and One Tales of the Arabian Nights*. Although its ceiling is flat, it is beautifully detailed and ingenious in its interlocking construction with ornaments in gold paint on a ground of blue and red. From this room one can walk out onto the portico enjoying the view of the hanging garden and the palm oasis.

On the terrace under the portico, the family can sit and relax over Arabic coffee or tea. The entrance also has openings to the right and to the left. The access on the left leads to the reception room; while

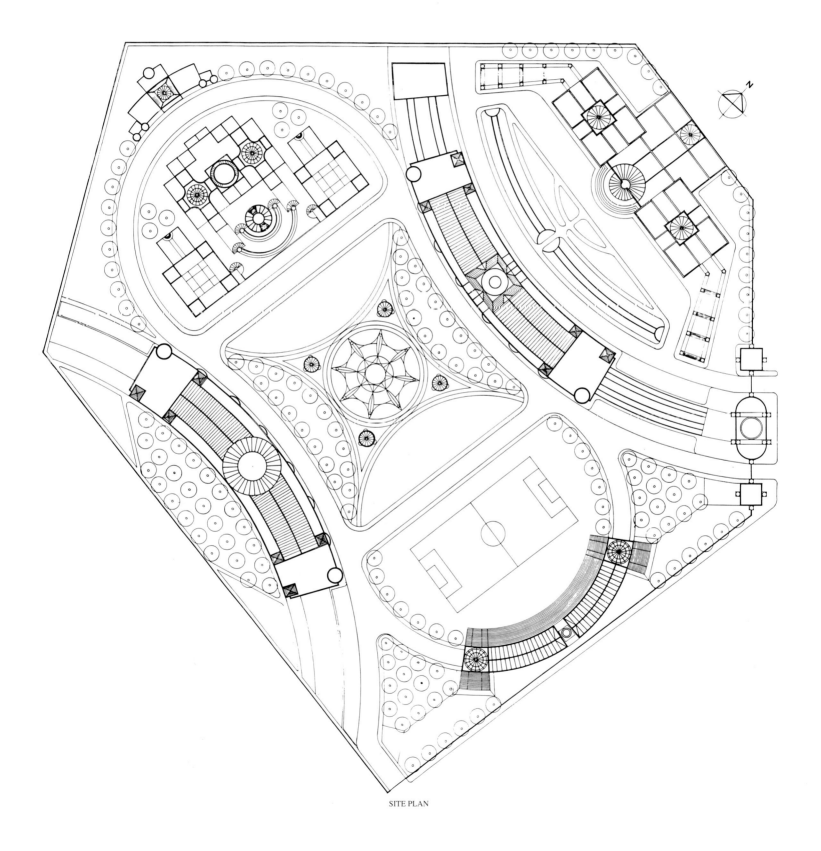

SITE PLAN

the one on the right leads to the dining room and living room. Over the door of the dining room there is a band of mosaic decoration. The inscription in the centre of it reads:

'Whatever you possess of this world comes from God'

The inscription on the other side, over the reception room, reads:

'Praises (be given) to God for His bestowing on us the benefit of our religion'

The entrance hall has two spacious staircases leading to the first floor, which in turn leads to the Blessing Room where the owner appears to the outside world. This hall is a square twelve metres and ten metres high from the floor to the apex of the central dome which is situated directly under the Moon Garden (Hadikat Al Qamar). The hall is impressive by the arrangement and symmetry of its detail. Panels of writing on each side of the square have the same inscription which reads:

'O God: thine is the praise forever, and thine are thanks forever'

The interior decoration of this room reflects the surroundings of the palace: palm trees with clusters of golden dates, various grasses and flowers. Waterfalls and lakes adorn the tapestries and paintings which are hung in the room. The door to the Baraka Room has two columns on either side. On the capital of each column there is an inscription. The inscription on the left column reads:

'There is no deity but God'
'Durability is God's glory to God'

And on the capital of the right column the inscription reads:

'There is no power or strength but in God'

The door has two leaves. Each leaf has three panels with the inscriptions:

'God help him'
'Glory to God'
'God is eternal'

The calligraphy blends with the design of the door and complements the classical order.

On the first floor, the small hall near the two staircases leads to alcoves of divans, one to the left and one to the right. These alcoves lead to the sleeping quarters. The one to the left is the master bedroom for the owner and the one to the right is another large bedroom for his wife. There is a plinth with flower vases on top, on either side of the door and at either end of each divan.

The ceilings of the left and right halls have similar characteristics to the other ceilings. There is a crown with a dome of the most elaborate pattern which is supported at either end by pendentives. They have a very curious mathematical construction and the result

is astonishing. It is here that East and West meet: the classical order of the West and the mathematical order of the East. This combination creates a powerful effect by the repetition of the most simple elements.

Between the sleeping room and the elegant small salon, where the bathers undress, there is a square space encompassing the shower room and the bathroom which are both paved with white marble. Light pours in through openings in the ceiling.

In the bathroom there is a semi-circular, arched niche with an inscription which reads:

'And be not one of the negligent'

The sleeping quarter has its own terrace where the owner and his wife can enjoy an unobstructed view; it is even possible to watch the football matches from the terraces by using binoculars.

The third level of the palace is the roof and from there one can reach the Moon Garden (Hadikat Al Qamar). This garden has several palm trees. It is here that the family can sit and enjoy the breeze sweeping across the landscape and look out onto the Al Nakheel Garden. Whilst sitting under the palms, the owner can see the whole city while dining with his family.

Just before the Moon Garden is a circular wall with two staircases. The inscriptions on the walls leading to the garden read:

'Wherein the warm gate descends to mitigate the cold winter, thereby producing salubrious air and mild temperature'

'Truly, so many are the beauties of every king that enfold, that even the stars in heaven borrow their light from us'

The Moon Garden, as stated previously, crowns the palace, as the palace crowns the other gardens on the ground floor. This is the hanging garden (Al Hadaik Al Mualakah).

This garden is like an open air theatre with a series of green backdrops at different levels. It contains the fountain of the swan, which is a circular form with various levels. Its waterfalls and steps, columns and walls are faced with marble reliefs in the form of animations which are reflected in the water.

The swans at the top of the first level are carved from white marble. The inscription around the basin reads:

'Blessed is he who gave a mansion which in its beauty exceeds all other mansions'

On the lower floor of the main villa are special companion quarters which include a reception, living rooms, dining rooms and four bedrooms. They are located to the left of the lower floor.

To the right of the lower floor is the private saloon with a reception, living and dining room and other services. Its windows open onto the main garden.

There are two smaller villas lower down the hill, one of which is for boys and the other for girls. Although these two villas are simple, they have very specific qualities. The elevations of the three villas have elegant proportions which blend perfectly with the landscape.

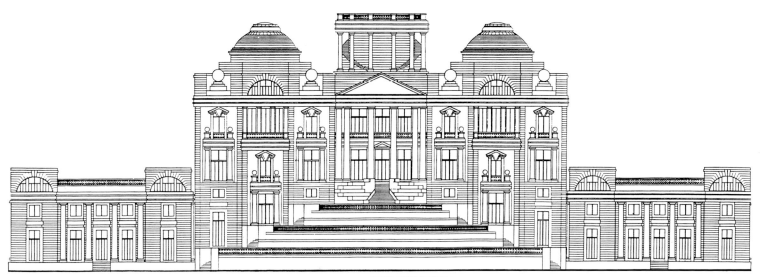

ROOF PLAN AND ELEVATION OF VILLA

The Sons' Villa

The plan of this villa consists of a central area and two side areas. The central area on the ground floor houses the reception hall, and the two side areas house the living and dining areas, while the first floor houses all the bedrooms and games rooms. The basement has a cinema with full projection equipment for twenty to thirty people. To the left of this building is the daughters' villa.

The Daughters' Villa

The girls' villa has the same type of layout and plan, and also has a cinema on the lower floor.

Children's Sleeping Quarters

At the far end of the villa complex is a curved building. This houses the children's sleeping quarters. The ground floor incorporates a reception room, a living room, a dining room and also games rooms, whilst the first floor has bedroom suites for the children; the lower ground floor provides bedroom suites for the nannies. At the other end of the children's sleeping quarters and directly opposite them is the football ground.

The Football Ground

The football ground has a regulation size pitch and standard sports amenities. A special gymnasium and exercise quarters are housed on the top floor which also has central viewing towers.

The Car Park

The roads which pass directly in front of the recreation building (C), the main reception and banqueting hall (B) lead straight to the car park, which is located underneath the football ground (H). This car park is on two levels and can accommodate four hundred cars. It also has a small workshop, maintenance shops, spare parts' store and equipment service shops.

Al Nakheel Garden

There are two gardens on either side of this building which give it the appearance of a natural stage set. The main section leads to the Rayhan Garden, and the private section leads to the Al Nakheel Gardens, which have a romantic fish pond. This pond differs in character from the others. The decoration is based on an imitation of natural vegetation and the total form is an imitation of animal shapes. There are eight fish carved in white marble. The mouldings are indicated by a faint line in gold. The Al Nakheel Gardens also contain a bird sanctuary consisting of four hand-crafted metal bird cages.

Main Section: Saloon and Recreation Area

This building is distinguished stylistically with distinctive elements. It consists of side wings, a central hall and a rear section. The interior of the entrance is characterised by a vast hall inspired by the houses of the ancient Romans. The whole complex has spacious rooms.

The building is raised and has steps in front of the facade. Here the circular columned arch appears to be crowned by two half domes, one bigger than the other. The area between the bigger and smaller dome has windows, which allow light to penetrate the building, thereby heightening the refined outline of the interior.

The two side wings have similar characteristics. They have two floors housing the swimming pool and gymnasium on one side, and the squash court and tennis court on the other.

The first floor of each wing is approached by a monumental flight of steps which leads eventually to the portico at each end of the building.

The entire complex possesses a sense of majestic nobility as a result of its architectural elements, such as the elegant balustrades, the curves of the wide staircase and the precise symmetry in the arrangement of the rooms and landscape.

The magnificent central curve of this building, extending over two storeys, includes the domed hall which leads to the third section with the reception hall on the right, the saloon on the left and dining room at the far end of the complex crowned with a small single dome.

The wooden doors of the entrances to the three rooms have brass ribs filled with stained glass in various colours. These are embellished with inscriptions written by hand over the mosaics and around the doorway, which read:

'Glory be given to God'
'O God! Thine is the praise forever.
And thine are the thanks forever'

Al Rayhan Garden

In front of the recreational area is the Al Rayhan Garden. This has an array of different flowers and a musical fountain similar to those of the patterns from the Lord's melody.

Palm Oases

There are three palm oases within the complex. Oranges, papayas and grapes grow in abundance in all the gardens. The gardens have a gate with an archway. The inscription around the arch reads:

' . . . and yet I am not alone, for I overlook, in astonishment, a garden, the like of which no human eyes ever saw'

Basil Al-Bayati

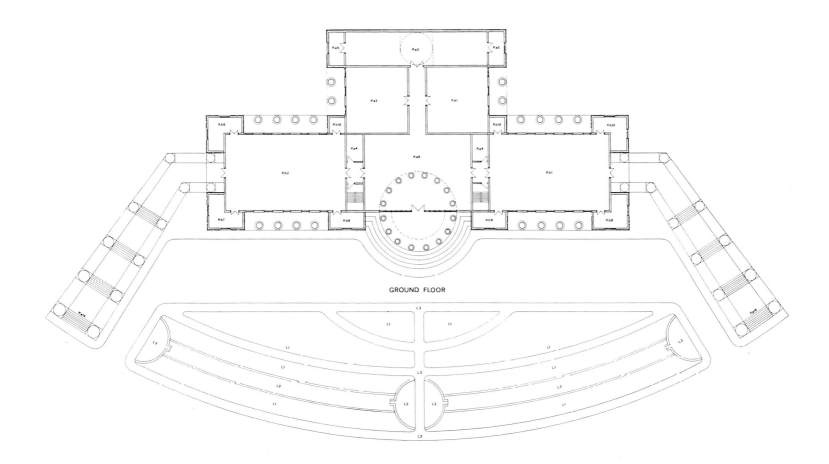

GROUND FLOOR

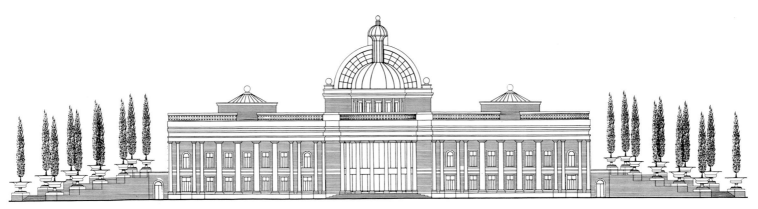

GROUND FLOOR PLAN AND ELEVATION OF DEVANIAH AND RECREATION AREA

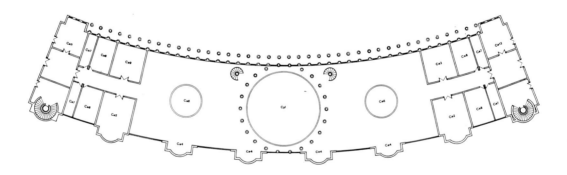

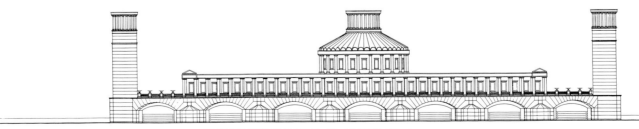

FIRST AND GROUND FLOOR PLANS AND ELEVATION OF FAMILY RECREATION AREA

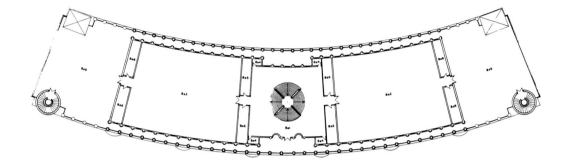

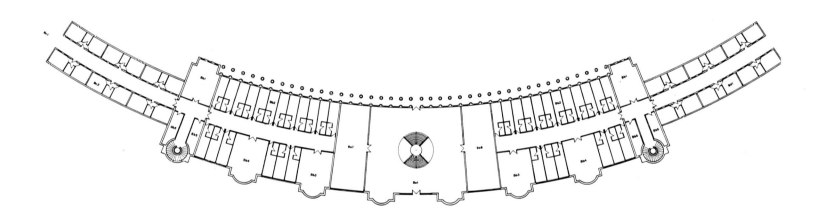

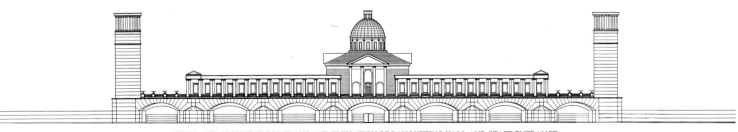

FIRST AND GROUND FLOOR PLANS AND ELEVATION OF BANQUETING HALL AND STAFF ENTRANCE

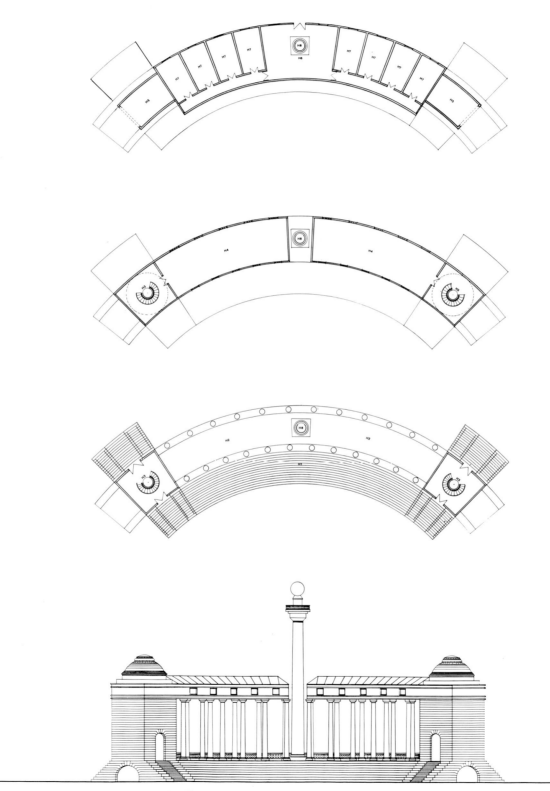

GROUND, TOP AND FIRST FLOOR PLANS AND ELEVATION OF FOOTBALL STAND

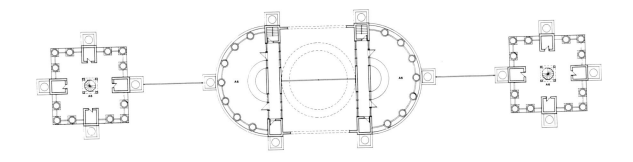

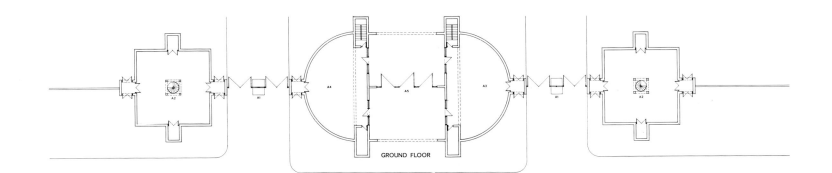

GROUND FLOOR

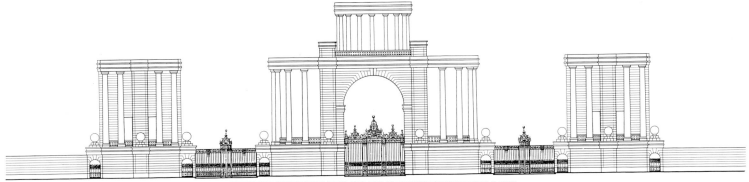

FIRST AND GROUND FLOOR PLANS AND ELEVATION OF ENTRANCE GATES

TV STUDIOS, VIDEO LIBRARY AND ADMINISTRATION BUILDING
ABU DHABI, UNITED ARAB EMIRATES, 1990

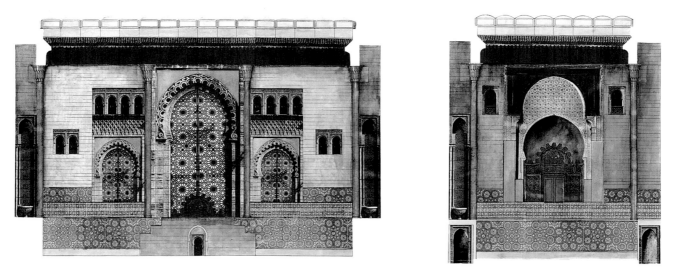

LONGITUDINAL ELEVATIONAL SECTION; CROSS ELEVATIONAL SECTION

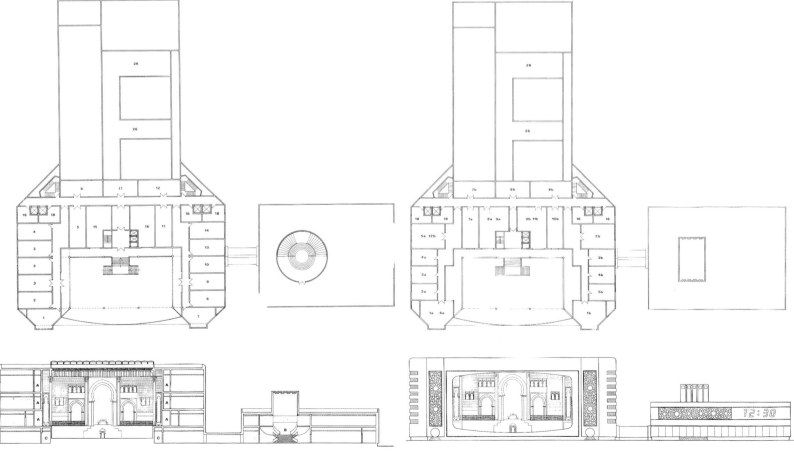

PERSPECTIVE; UPPER GROUND AND FIRST FLOOR PLANS; LONGITUDINAL SECTION; FRONT ELEVATION

QASIR GHUMDAN HOTEL

SANA'A, YEMEN, 1990

There is very little known about the ledgendary palace of Ghumdan. The following chapter describes the palace as it is imagined by Basil Al-Bayati. The new schemes of the Qasir Ghumdan Hotel project is based on this story.

Ghumdan was thought to be the world's first skyscraper; it was one of the thirty wonders of the world. The first to start building it was Sam, son of Noah (peace be on him), when he built Sana'a. It is also said that Sulieman, son of Dawood (peace be on them both), had a share in the construction. It was completed by Ass'ad Al-Kamel.

Ghumdan was regarded as Sana'a's first palace, and was both a centre for and a symbol of the supreme authority that dominated southern Arabia at that time. It was a place in which armies were mobilised and sent to remote lands. The inhabitants of that palace were healthy and strong; whoever lived there never knew disease and the women always looked young. Its floor was made of sulphur and thus no harmful insects could survive.

Ghumdan Palace was square-shaped, its length being equal to its width. It was situated on the top of a mountain, with an entrance cut through the rocks at the base; God Almighty had made each mountain in this world with veins inside it. There were twenty ceilings stretching from top to bottom of that mountain and the palace had three other floors cut into it. The lower floors were dedicated to visitors while the upper ones were the living quarters. There were four different facades: one built with white stone, another with black stone, the third with green and the remaining with red. Its corners were guarded by towers of the same colour. A fence with one gate surrounded the palace. The top of the fence had battlements and towers.

Inside the palace were open halls overlooked by every floor except the upper room of Ghumdan, which was known as Bilqis Hall. This hall was eighty-eight metres high. In the middle of it, on the ground, lay a big clock used to calculate the hours each day. The Himyiris were the first to invent dropping clocks. Bilqis Hall had four exits. The first led to the gate of the hall dug into the mountain. The second had ingenious stairs leading to a hall above which was a suspended pool. The remaining openings were windows, one overlooking a palm tree, the other a waterfall. The ceiling of that room was made of sixty-four pieces of marble. Each piece contained pieces of copper within which candles were fixed at varying distances from each other. These candles gave full lighting at night to all the corridors overlooking the hall.

Those floors were connected to each other in four places by vertical stairs that could not be seen from inside the hall. There were also four horizontal surfaces that were pulled by ropes to carry people from one floor to another as if they were on a flying carpet, as in *A Thousand and One Tales of the Arabian Nights*. When seated on those 'flying surfaces' the visitors were able to see the palace gardens on the sides.

Each floor contained twenty-two rooms. Gold dominated all other colours in the decoration of the walls and ceilings of these rooms.

There was a special room that had a bed with seven hundred bases of green silk brocade covered with red rubies. On the lower floor was a large hall assigned to the women for their toilet. Over its entrance, the name of Lamis was engraved in marble and painted with gold. The walls and ceiling of this hall were covered with engravings, ornaments and mosaic work similar to the decorations found in the Alhambra Palace in Andalusia. It is said that those who built the Alhambra were the grandsons of the builders of Ghumdan Palace. In this hall the women applied kohl to their eyelids believing that, in addition to making them more attractive, it would protect their eyes from diseases.

Opposite Lamis Hall was another hall called Shams (Sun). Whoever entered that hall would come out refreshed and cured of any ills. On the right side were two entrances leading to two separate wings. Each wing was divided into two floors, and each floor contained ten rooms.

On the left side there were also two entrances leading to two halls. The secrets of these halls were unknown. It was said that the Lord of the palace used them for his private affairs. At the entrance were drawn images of the peacock, the master of the birds of Heaven. The lower floor was a place where people gathered on entering the palace.

The man in charge of the palace was strong and powerful. His countenance was fierce, and this was emphasised by his black beard and wide eyes. He wore beautiful clothes made of white silk held by a green belt embroidered with gold. In addition, he wore a turban also embroidered with gold. His orders were obeyed by all in the palace.

Around the main hall on the ground floor were shops full of jewels from Somalia and Zanzibar and others with an abundance of incense and silk from China. The signs above read from left to right as in Greek and Latin.

In addition to the exits in the middle of the hall, there were four exits in the corners that led to other halls. These halls witnessed a variety of activities: circles of learning, counsels of war and political debates. Two halls were reserved for banquets and people came from all over to enjoy the hospitality of the generous Lord of the palace.

The goat was a highly revered animal in those times, and this was reflected in the decoration of the hall. At the entrance to one of the halls there was a drawing of a goat. The tables were of the most beautiful marble with engravings on the edges in the shape of goats heads. The eating of meat was prohibited in that hall; instead, people were given vegetarian food and a variety of tropical fruits from trees brought from India, such as guava, tamarind and mango. The walls of the hall were covered with ornaments and drawings of fruits and vegetables.

There was another banqueting hall named after Shamar Bahrashr who was an important figure at the end of the third century and the beginning of the fourth century AD. During his reign, relations with the bedouins were strengthened. This hall had marble statues of winged and horned lions resembling those of Persia. Shamar was

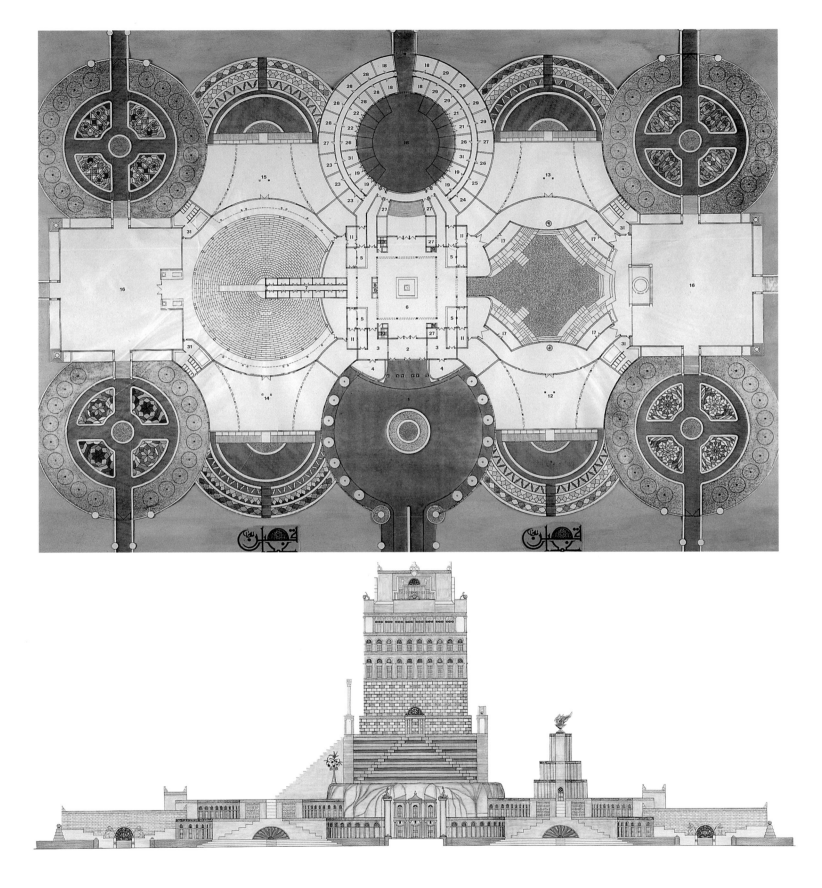

GROUND FLOOR PLAN AND FRONT ELEVATION

called Shamar the Winged, and it was he who subdued Persia. The ornaments on the walls and ceiling were influenced by Persian and Hellenistic art.

There was a large room at the top of the palace called Ghumdan Hall. It was a square room with rounded corners. The ceiling consisted of eight pieces of marble under which were eight terraces overlooking the interior of the room.

The hall had four doors, each facing a corner of the palace. In the middle of the ceiling was a dome. The middle terrace was oval, five metres in diameter and made of transparent green material. The light in that room could be seen from far away at night. The four doors, which faced the four points of the compass, were open towards the top of the room, and opposite the rounded corners were copper statues of lions with eagles' heads; the legs of each statue were inside the hall but the chest and head were outside the palace. Each was hollow between mouth and tail so that when the wind blew roaring noises were produced. In addition, there were curtains decorated with bells which chimed when the curtains were ruffled by a breeze. The sound of bells could be heard for miles. Charming gardens separated these lions and the walls of the hall. Anyone who walked through these gardens could see the whole city. The upper and lower sections of the walls were covered with teak and ebony.

Concerts of songs and music were held in the hall till daybreak The songs were repetitive and had a melancholy air. The female dancers wore long loose dresses and silver studded necklaces with jewels that sparkled as they moved. Their dresses were of embellished silk in beautiful colours, around which they fastened belts. The effect of luminosity and light was heightened further by the mirrored floor.

The oval ceiling had a copper crescent on top of it. The moon had good associations for the people there, especially with its splendid soft light which, when combined with the cool breeze during the night, brought comfort to the soul. That crescent was lit at night so that anyone looking at it from beneath the transparent oval ceiling would think that it was real. A garden called the Garden of the Palace surrounded the hall. Birds with white-ringed black necks would visit it in spring.

Ghumdan Palace was surrounded by a series of high towers which resembled those of the old Egyptian Kingdom. They had narrow vertical openings. There were two towers with pointed tops in the middle of each facade, whose corners were squared. They were cut out of the rock and had terraces with cylindrical towers crowned by copper lions. The palace had either round or oval-shaped windows and its walls were covered with white plaster and lined in brown.

A tree was planted in the mountain between two towers at one of the corners, with gushing waters of an unknown origin; some narrators say it stood as a memorial to the Campaign of the Water of Life. The water from this tree ran down the slopes of the mountain to its base where it gathered in the middle of four mountains to form a lake of sweet clear water in which fish could be seen. The tide was a remarkable phenomenon in that lake for it ebbed and flowed unceasingly at every season. The water had the effect of suppressing men's sexual desires whilst doing the opposite to women. The water would stop gushing at sunset causing the lake to dry up. When the lake was dry, a huge rock four metres high used to appear; no one knew where the rock disappeared during the day for its height was greater than the depth of the water. The rock would rise gradually as the level of the water decreased. Every day, different words appeared engraved in the rock which actually shone in the moonlight.

There was a large opening under the palace through the mountain and under the tree. Anyone looking at the water running down from the spring would have thought that the tree was weeping out of grief.

The lake was surrounded by four mountains with slopes that were turned into graded fields separated by stone walls built on the edges. Many species of birds inhabited that area, including the nightingale, hoopoe and lark.

On the other side of the palace stood a palm tree called Alyania'a Suhook which had leaves extending inside the palace. Visitors could see the palm tree from all floors. The palm tree is one of consequence; it is narrated that Adam used to drink from the clouds and when his hair and nails grew long Archangel Jibril came to him, cut his hair and trimmed his nails then buried them in the earth. God then made a palm tree grow in that place. Below that tree was a circular courtyard surrounded by huge columns; in its centre was the Rayhan Garden full of different kinds of roses and aromatic plants.

There were gardens, stretching from the sixth floor down to the Rayhan Gardens, filled with many different kinds of trees. The gardens on the front facade extended to the top of the mountain then inclined left on the slope towards the big gate cut in the middle of the rock; resembling the gate found in the Petra Tombs.

The palace was on top of a mountain surrounded by four other mountains. Those, in turn, were surrounded by gardens called Uzala which had eighty canals extending to the outer fence of the palace. One of those gardens at the back of the palace terminated in a pyramid covering a cylindrical building as an extension to the mountain on which the palace was erected. That building ended in a half-cylindrical shape with oval openings in its lower section and cylindrical columns in the upper end. The Europeans later adopted that style of building for their places of worship.

It is said that the cylindrical and pyramid-shaped building contained many wonders. One of the narrators claims that before the pyramid-shaped cover was built, the mountain extended over that place; and there was a cave which had inside it one of the rare treasures of the Arabian Peninsula: a spring of clear hot water. If people with diseases immersed themselves in its water they emerged cured. One day the ceiling of that cave fell in causing the water to splash into the air forming a Flying Lake. People used to visit that lake and sit beneath it watching those who were swimming without any drop of water falling on their heads. As a result, the Lord of the palace ordered that the pyramid ceiling be built and that a ship be constructed on its summit. When on board he felt like the captain of a flying ship. He ate fish there with his suite once a week.

At the entrance was a wide circular yard with a fountain in the centre. At the front of the yard were two columns on top of which were two fishes which had glittering eyes and a stone in their mouths called *Yaliht*. Anyone who touched the stone on entering the court of the Lord of the palace would have his request granted.

On the front facade the graduated stone gardens ended in the heads of animals with the horns of mountain goats. These were believed to ward off evil spirits.

Basil Al-Bayati

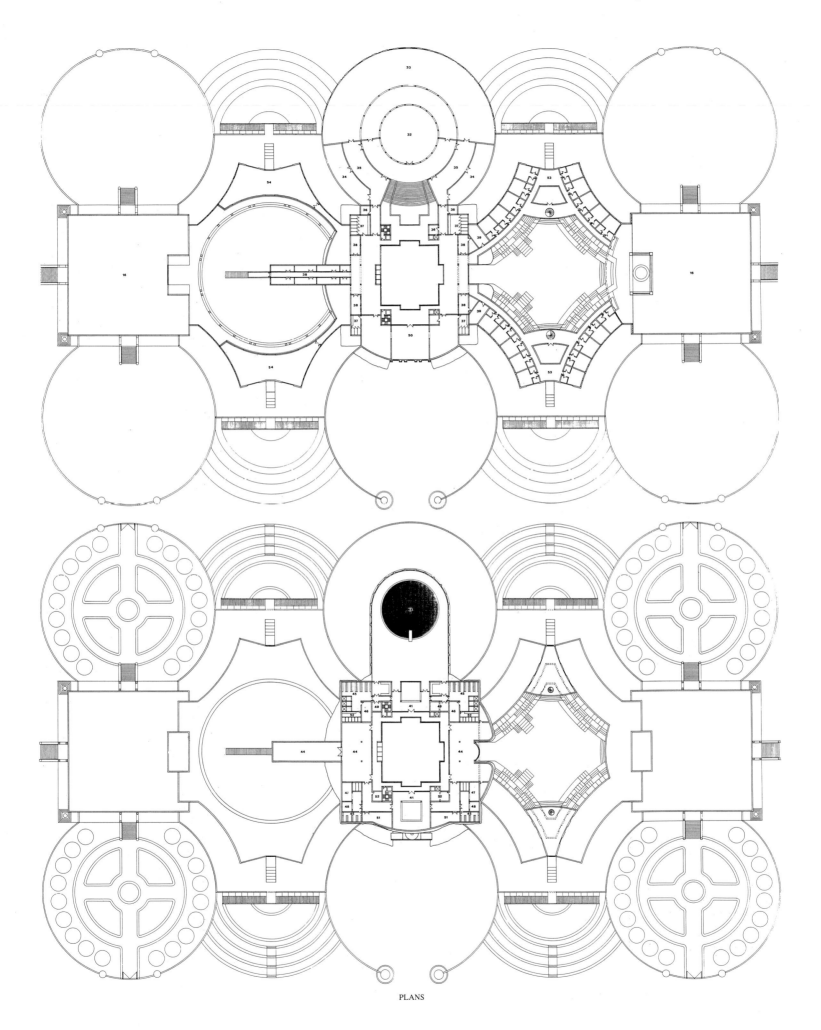

PLANS

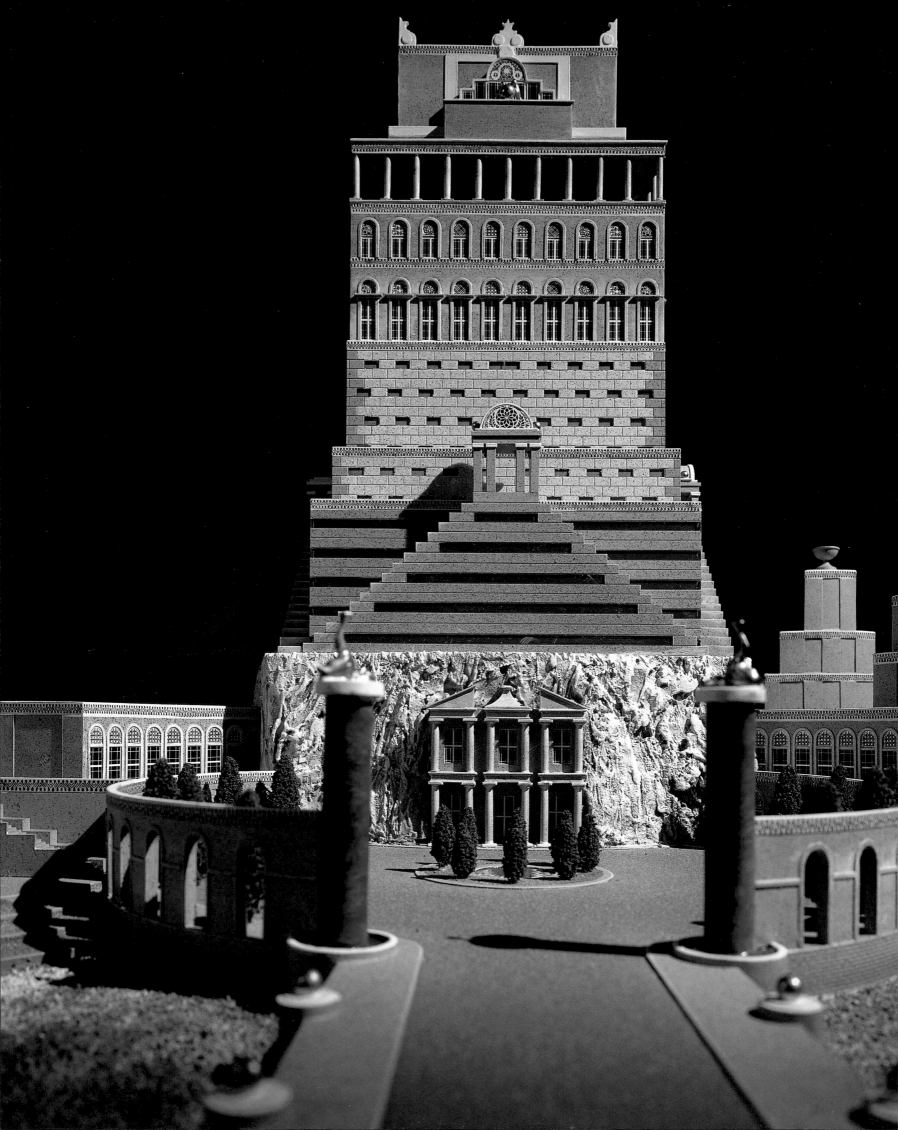

OPPOSITE: QASIR GHUMDAN HOTEL; *ABOVE:* SITE PLAN AND BACK ELEVATION

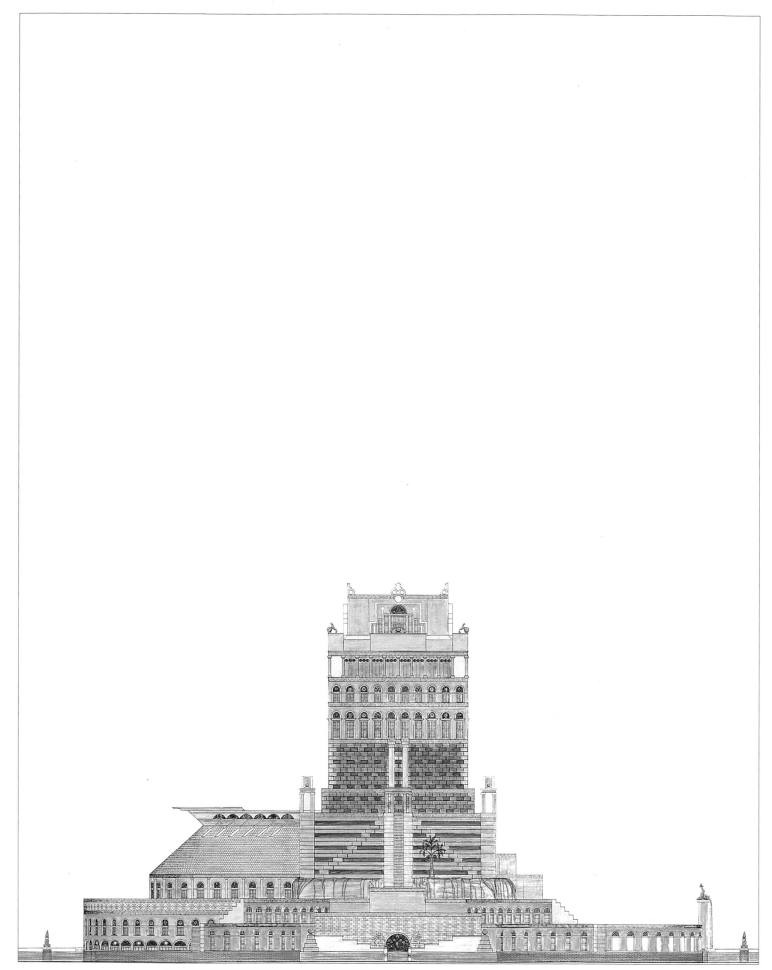

ELEVATION; *OPPOSITE:* PERSPECTIVES OF COURTYARD AND SWIMMING POOL; *FOLLOWING PAGES:* OVERALL VIEW

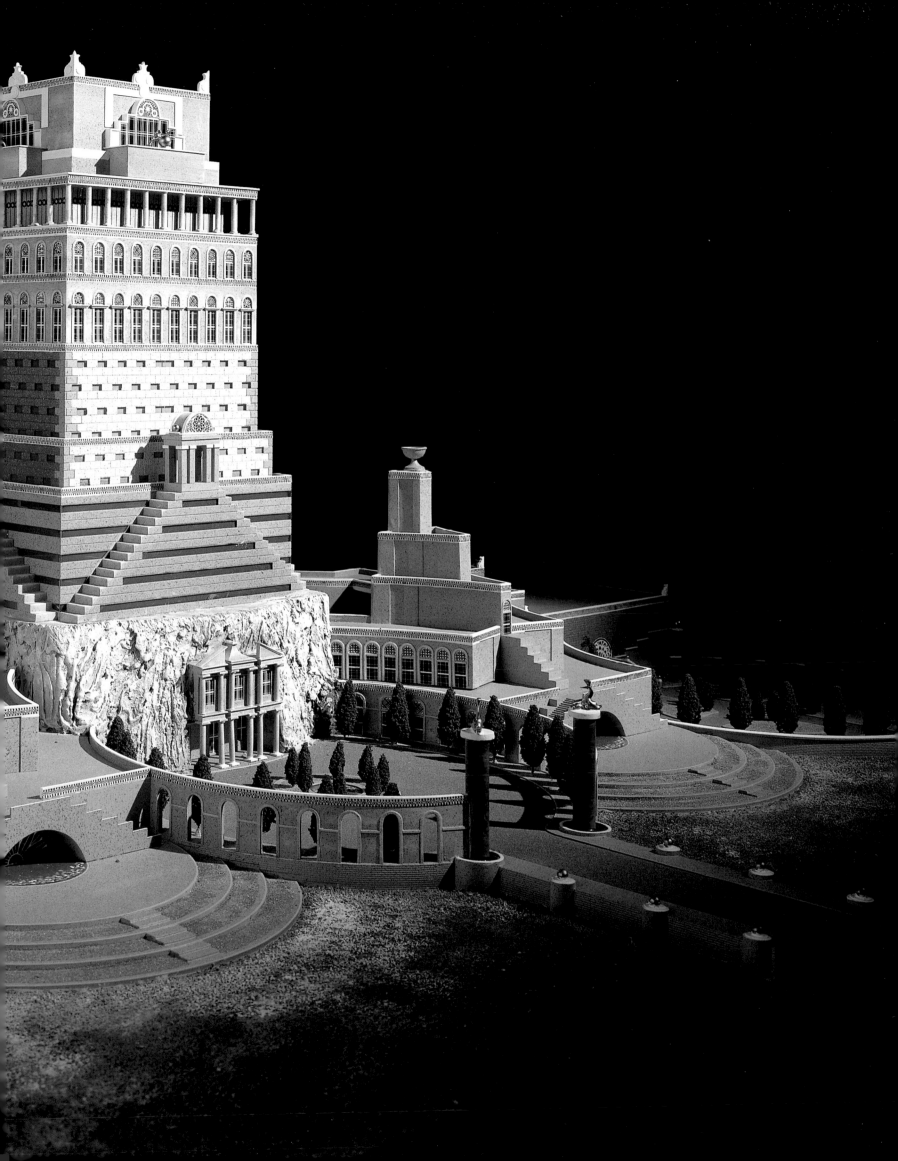

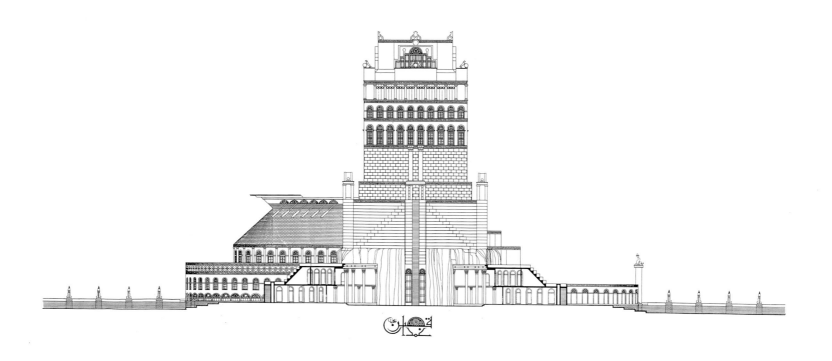

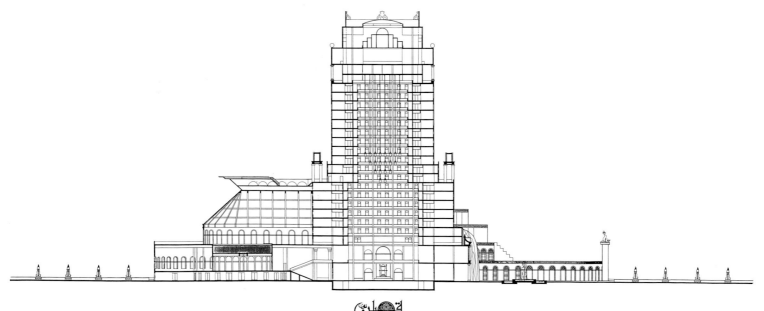

SECTIONS THROUGH COURTYARD AND ATRIUM

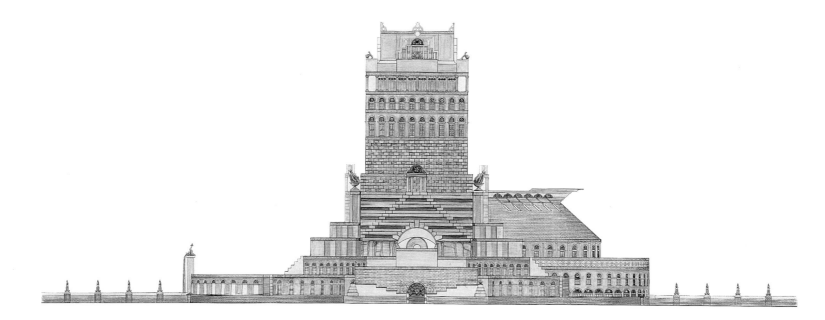

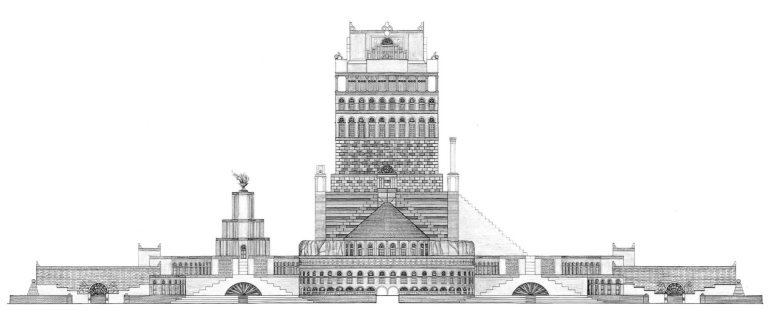

SIDE AND BACK ELEVATIONS; *FOLLOWING PAGES:* OVERALL VIEW

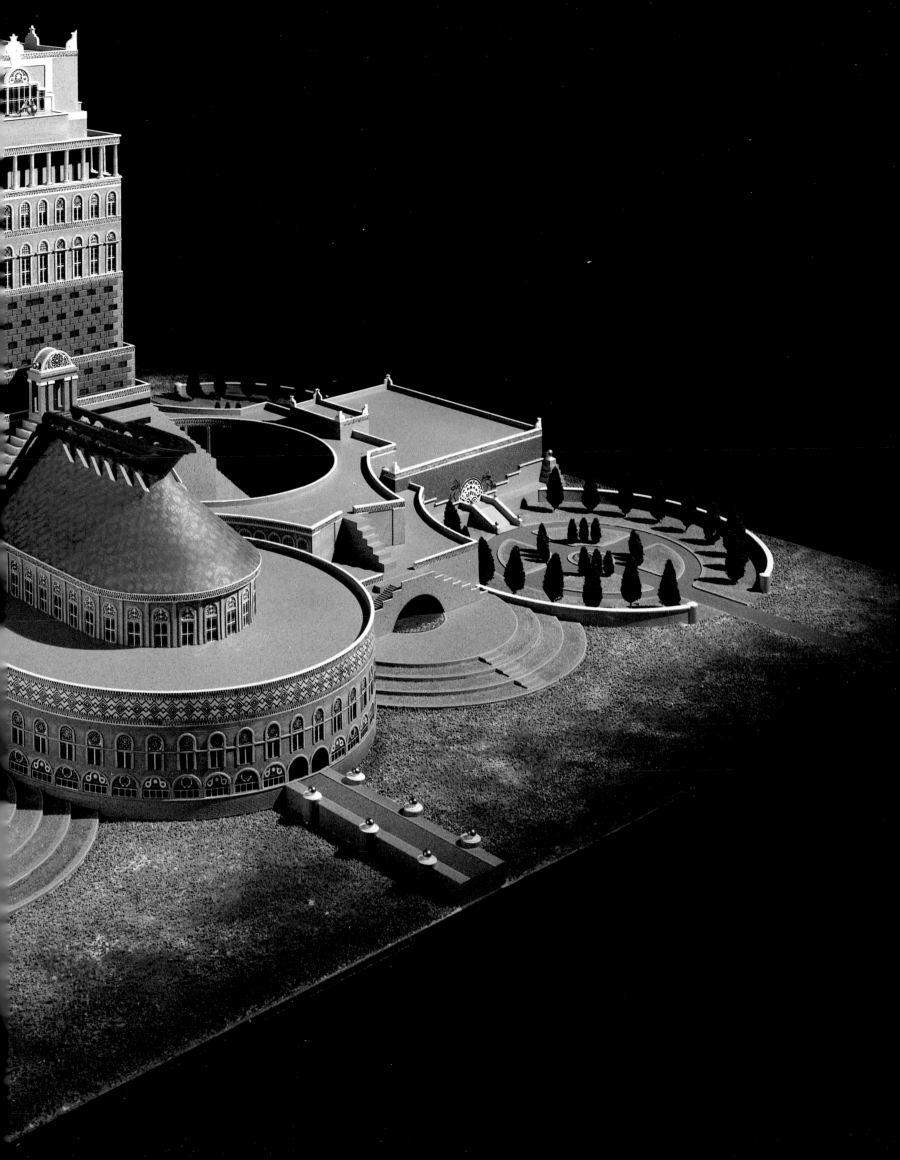

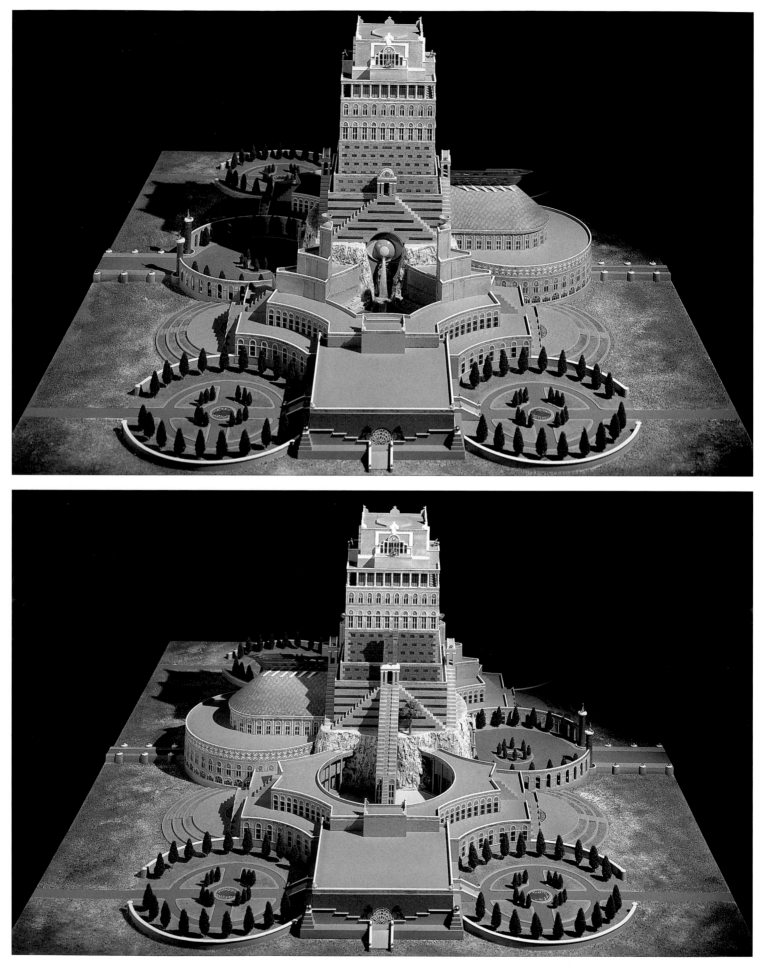

SIDE VIEWS OF MODEL AT HIGH LEVEL

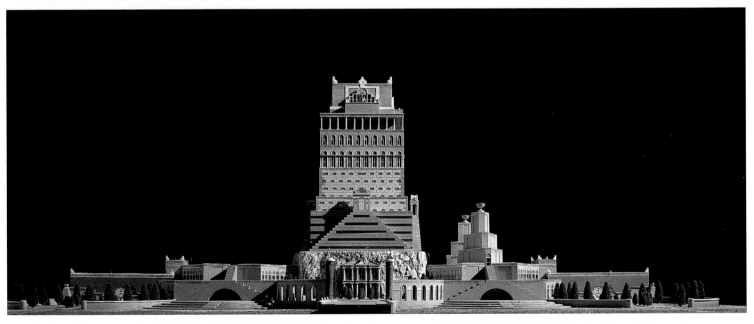

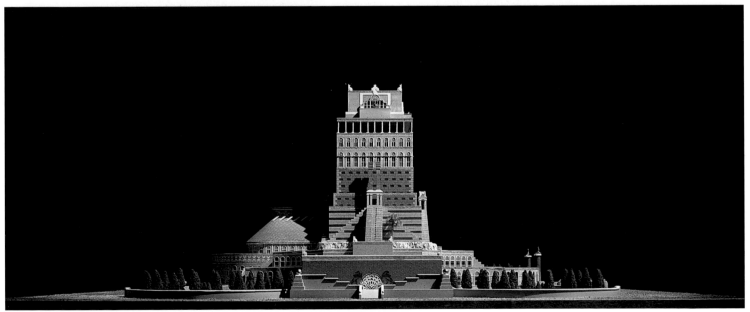

SIDE VIEWS OF MODEL AT LOW LEVEL

91

DAKKAH PROJECT, MAALLA

ADEN, YEMEN, 1990

SIDE ELEVATION AND TYPICAL PLAN

GROUND FLOOR PLAN AND FRONT ELEVATION

TRADE CENTRE

BUDAPEST, 1990

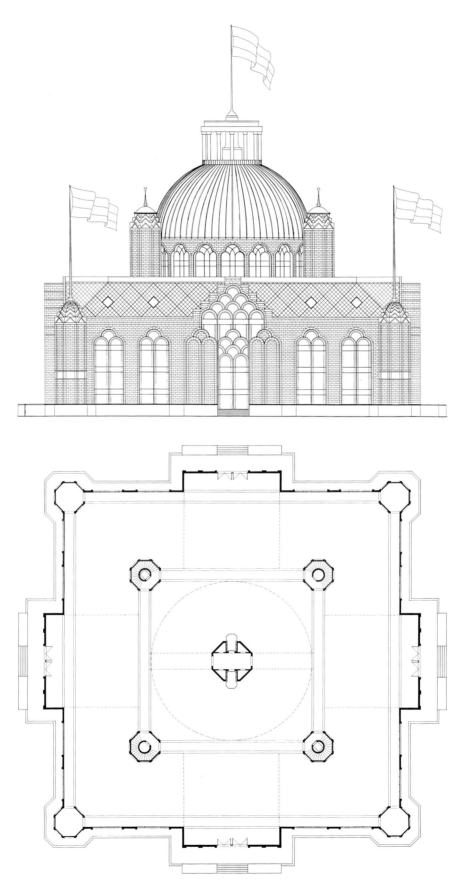

ELEVATION AND GROUND FLOOR PLAN

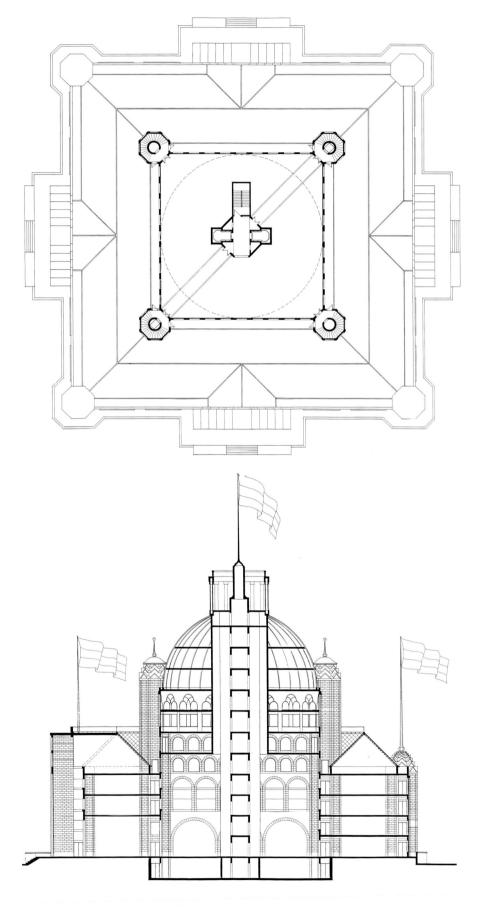

CROSS SECTION AND SIXTH FLOOR PLAN

27 – 30 NICOLSON SQUARE

EDINBURGH, SCOTLAND, 1990

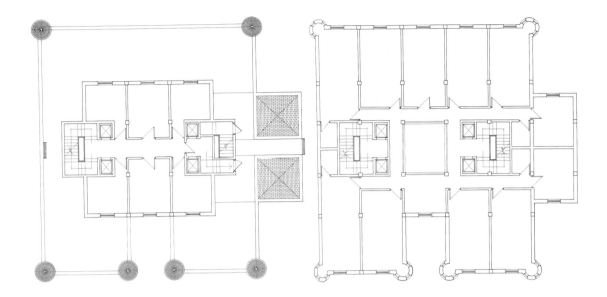

SECOND, THIRD, FIFTH AND SIXTH FLOOR PLANS; ELEVATION FROM NICOLSON SQUARE

THE DRIVE, ICKENHAM

MIDDLESEX, 1991

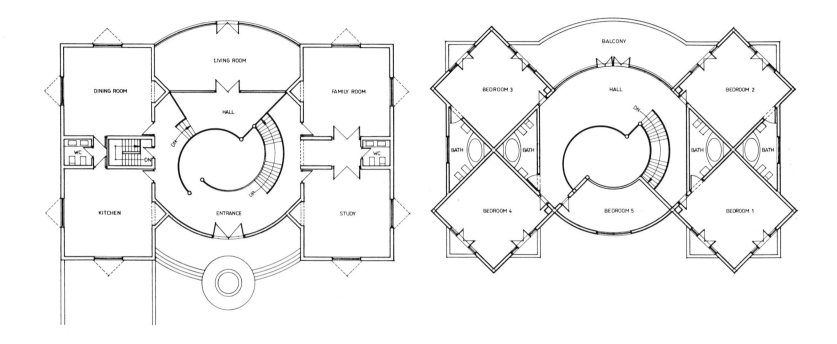

GROUND AND FIRST FLOOR PLANS; PROPOSED ELEVATIONS

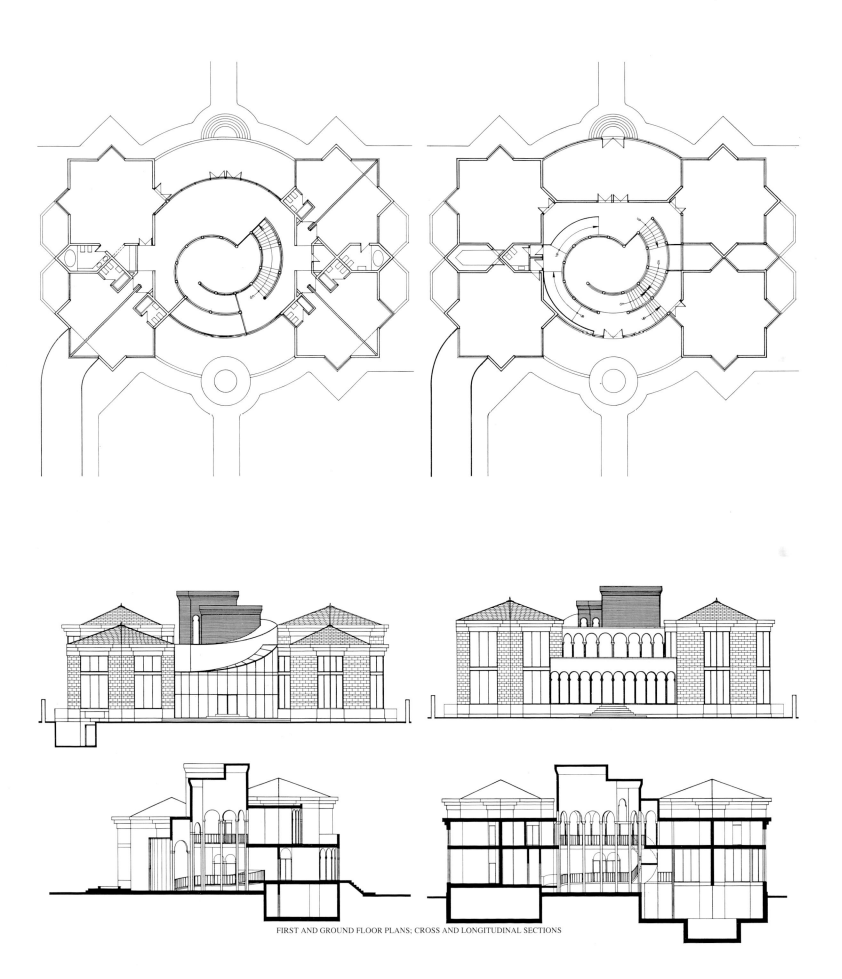

FIRST AND GROUND FLOOR PLANS; CROSS AND LONGITUDINAL SECTIONS

SEASIDE COMPLEX

ADEN, YEMEN, 1991

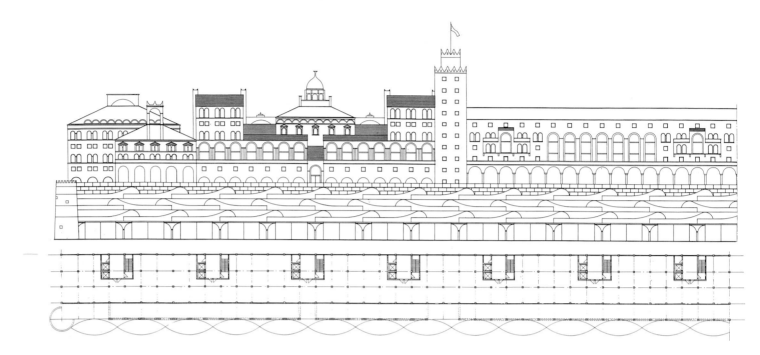

PART PLANS AND ELEVATIONS OF THE COMPLEX

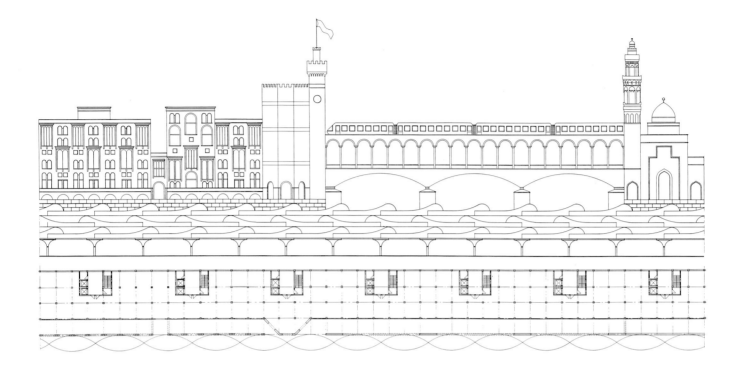

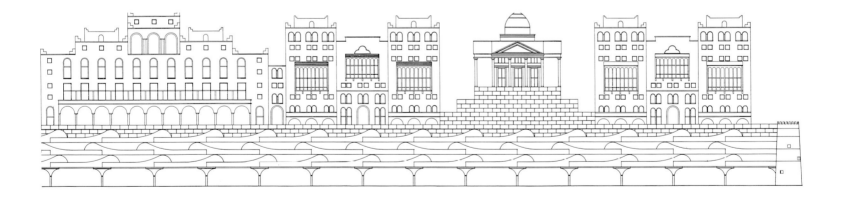

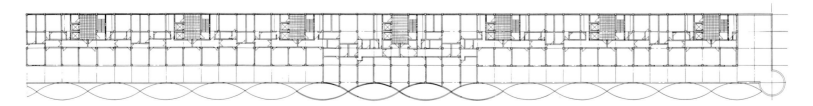

PART PLANS AND ELEVATIONS OF THE COMPLEX

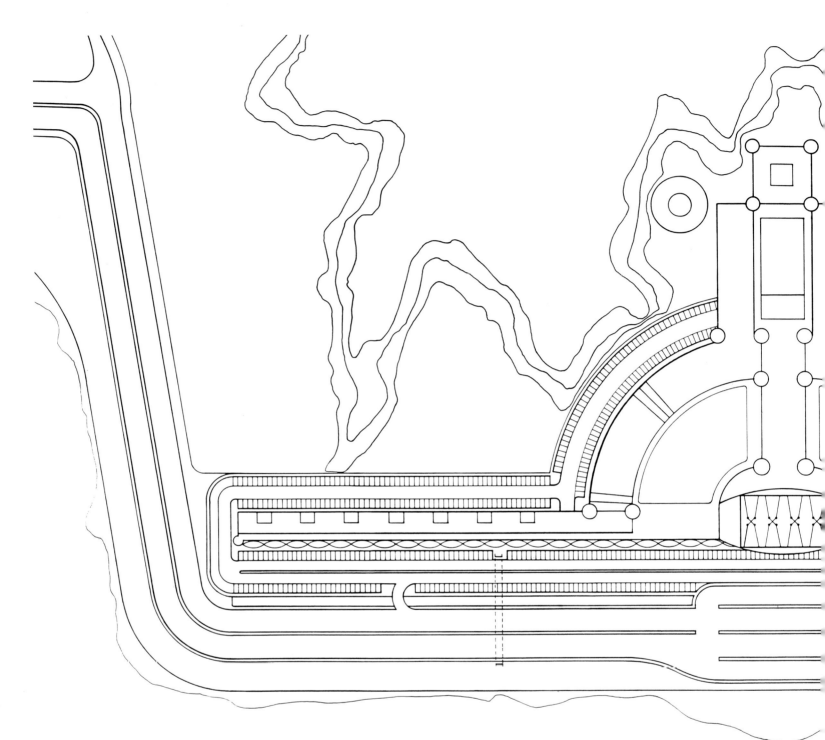

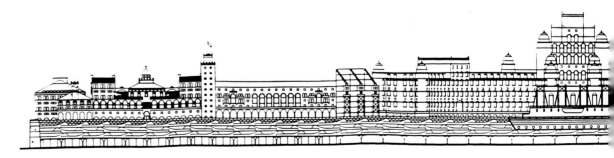

SITE PLAN AND SITE ELEVATION

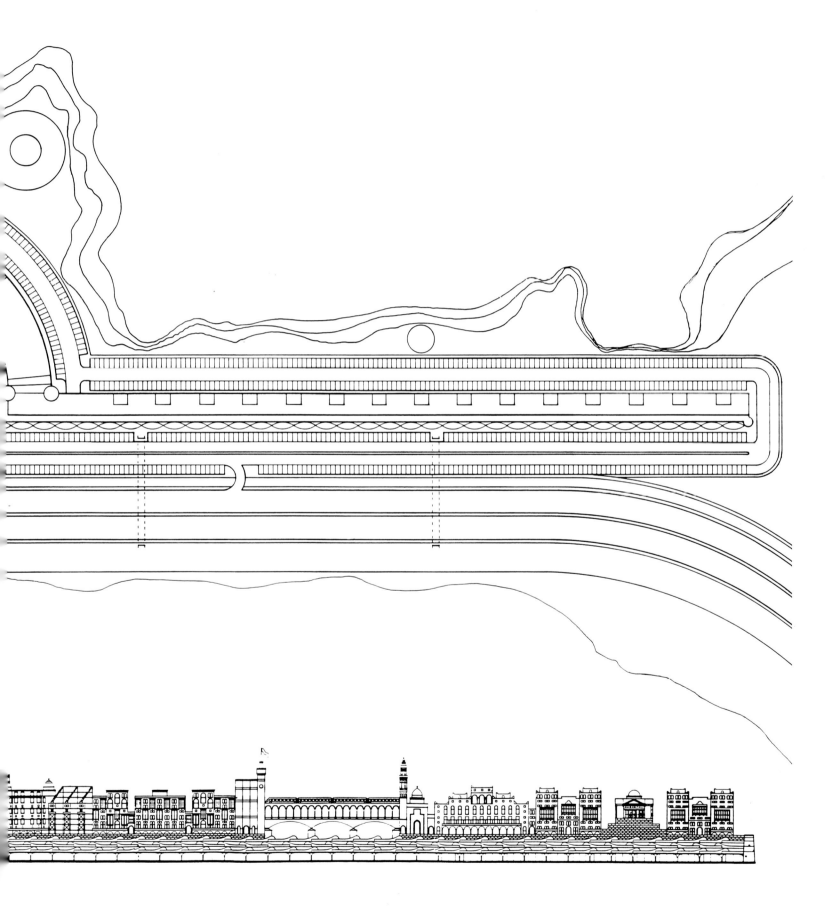

ST CROSS ROAD, OXFORD
STUDENT ACCOMMODATION, 1991

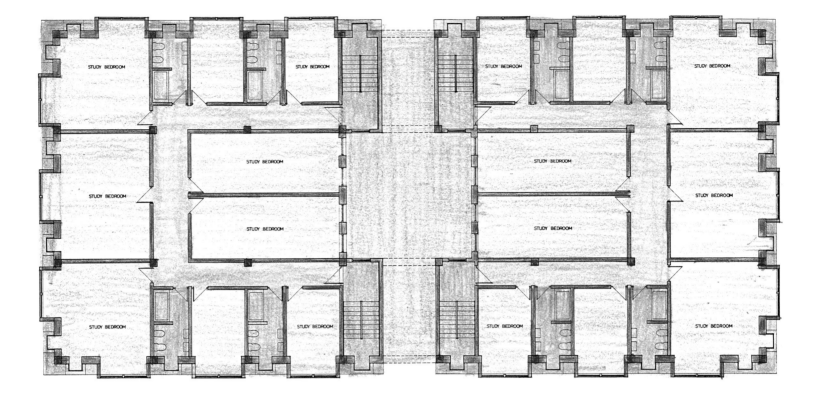

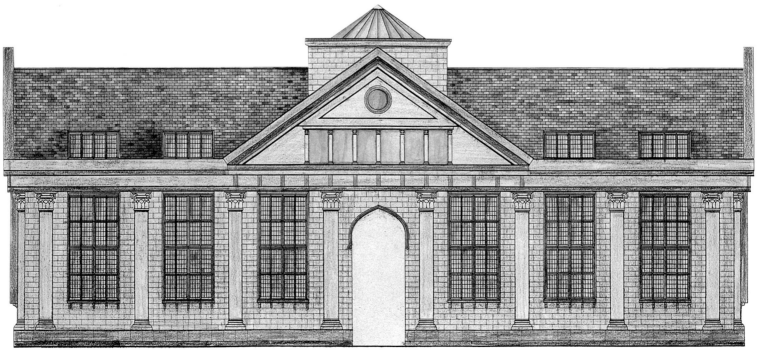

FIRST AND SECOND FLOOR PLANS; FRONT ELEVATION

COLLEGE FOR ISLAMIC STUDIES
OXFORD, 1991

MANOR ROAD

HOLY CROSS CEMETERY

ST CROSS CHURCH

HOLY CROSS CEMETERY

ALLOTMENT GARDENS

MAGDALEN GROVE - DEER PARK

SITE PLAN

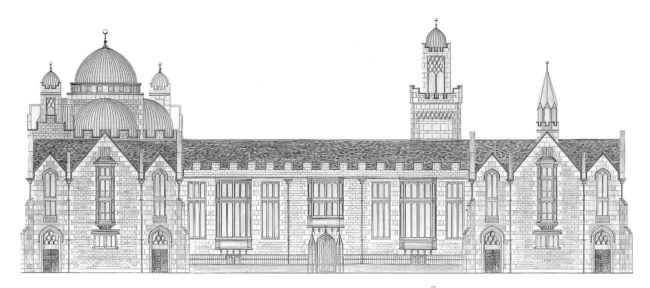

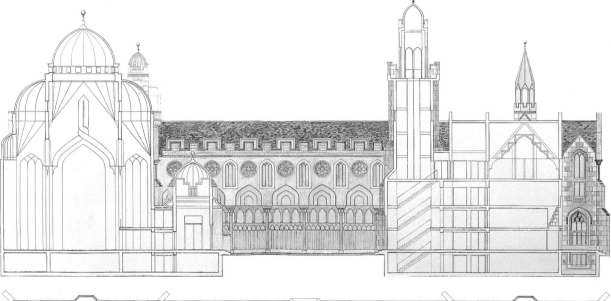

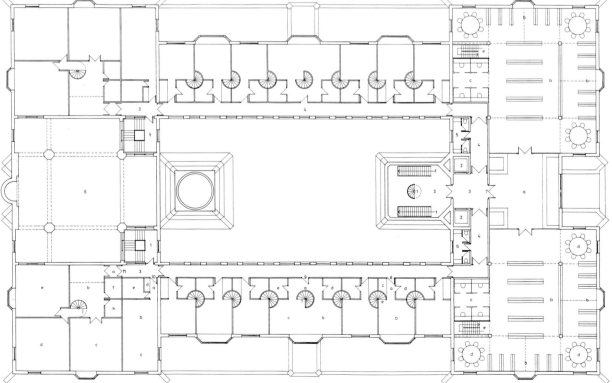

ELEVATION OF MIHRAB AND SECTION THROUGH COURTYARD TOWARDS THE MOSQUE; SECOND FLOOR PLAN; *OPPOSITE:* AERIAL VIEW OF MODEL

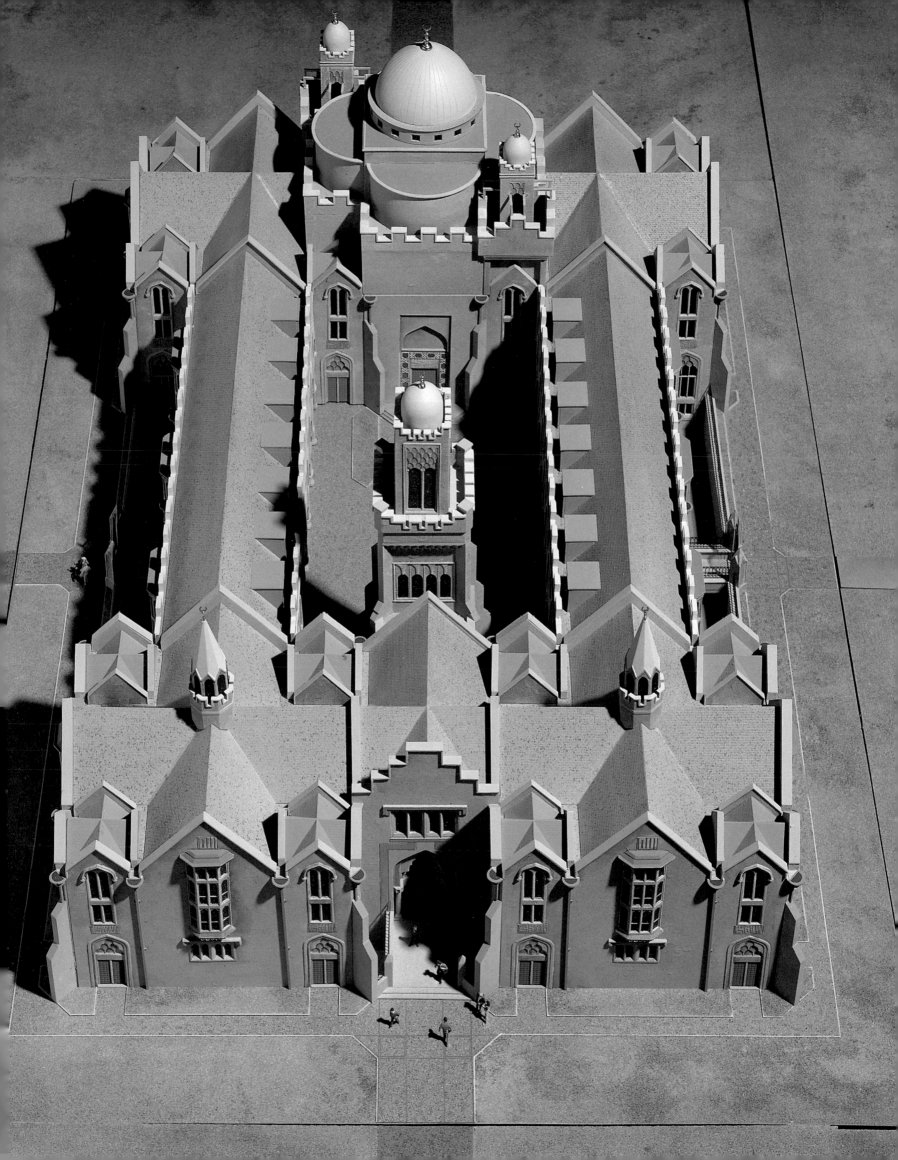

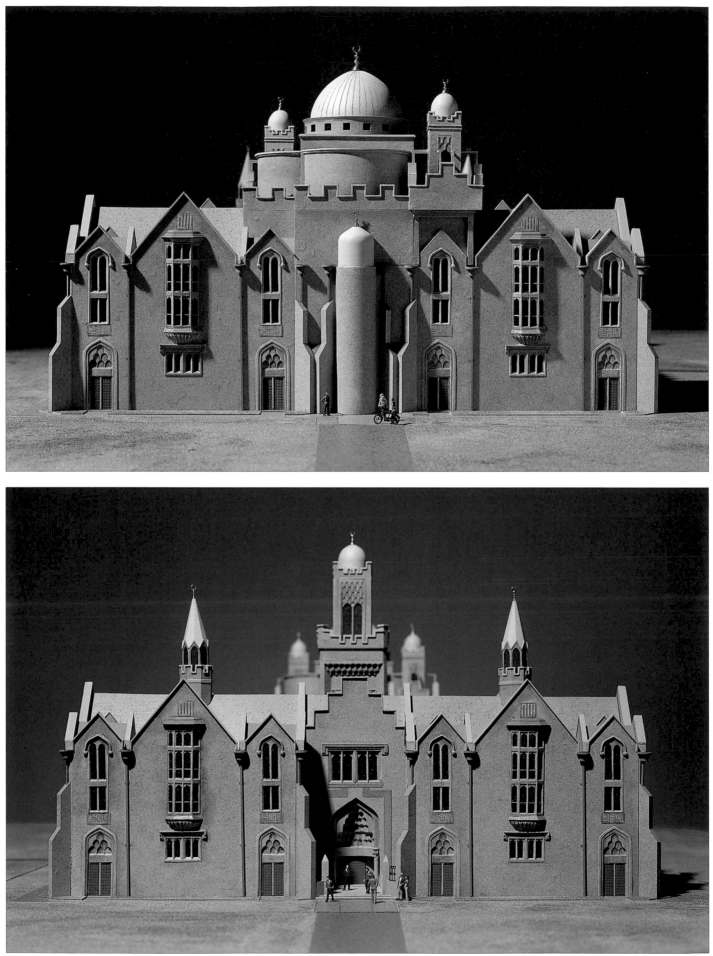

PHOTOGRAPHS OF MODEL SHOWING MIHRAB AND FRONT OF THE BUILDING; *OPPOSITE:* PHOTOGRAPHS OF MODEL SHOWING COURTYARD

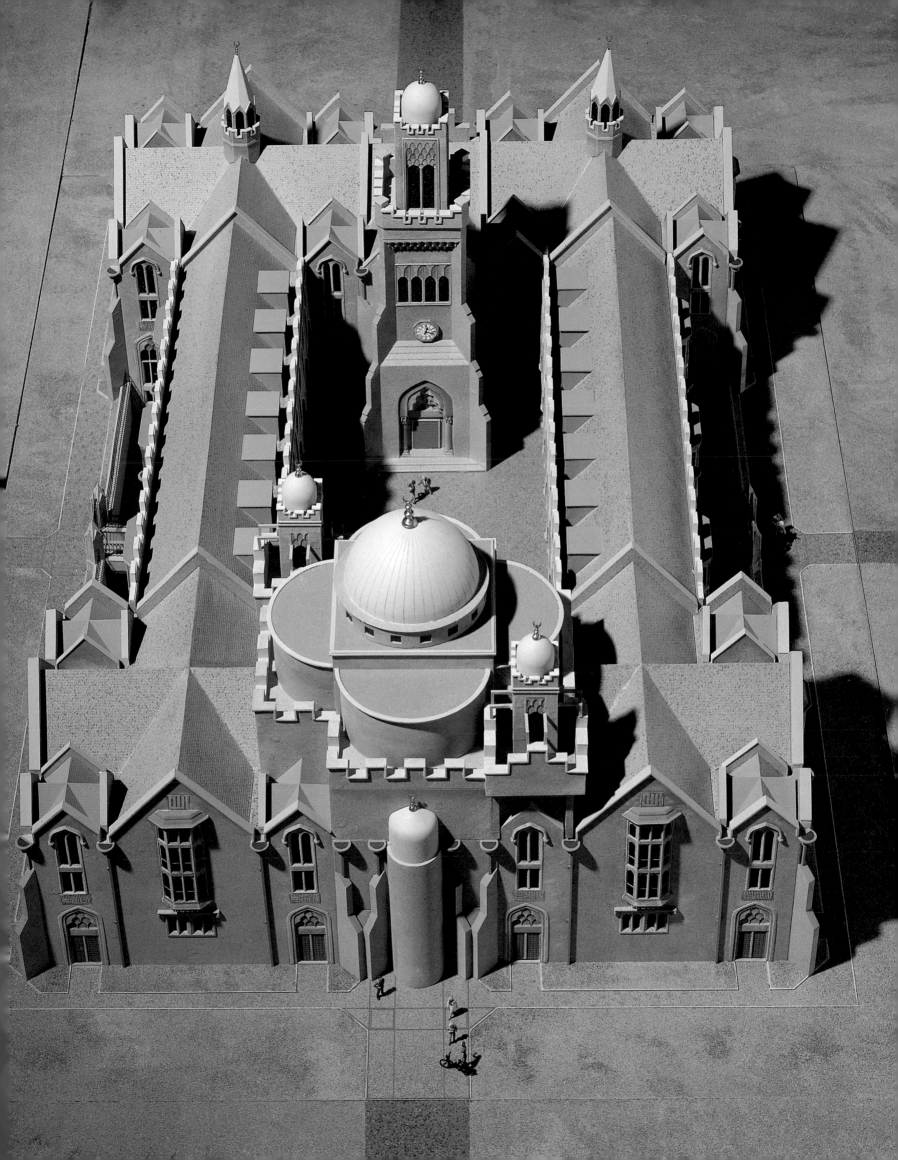

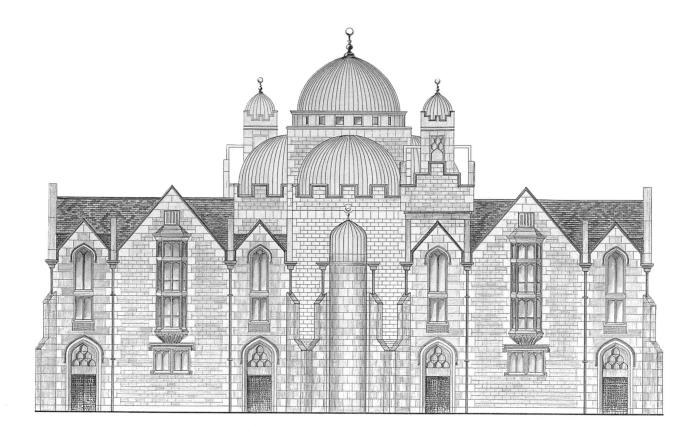

ELEVATION OF MIHRAB AND SECTION THROUGH COURTYARD TOWARDS THE MOSQUE

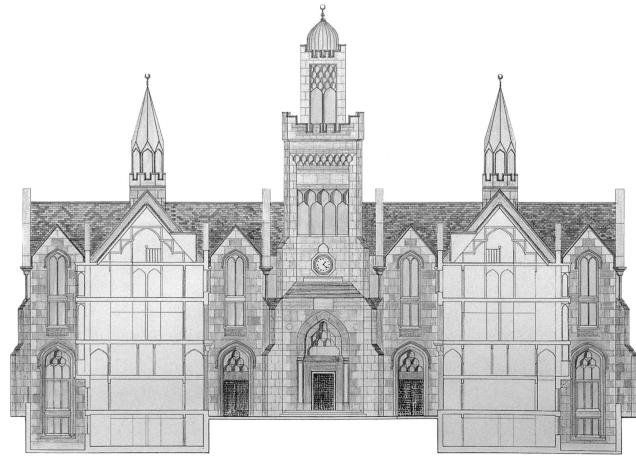

FRONT ELEVATION AND CROSS SECTION TOWARDS MINARET

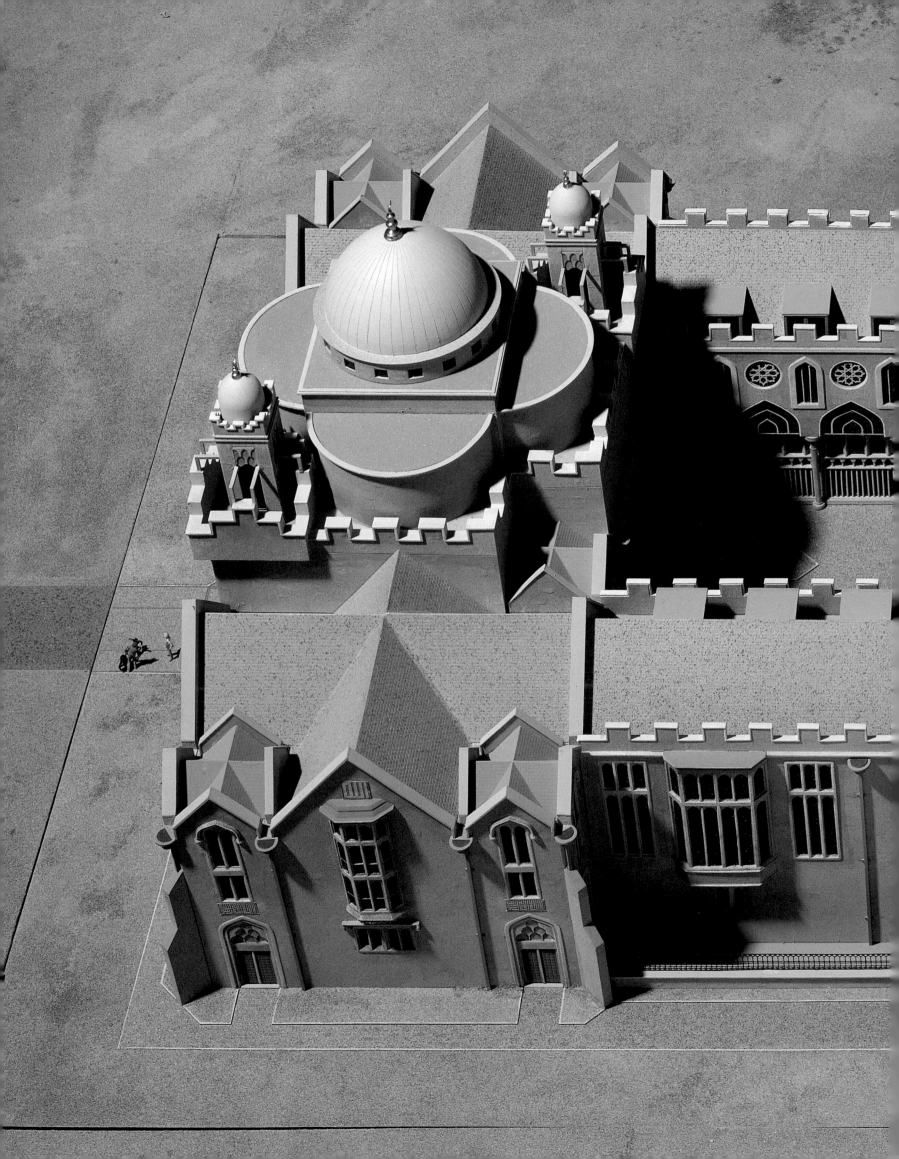

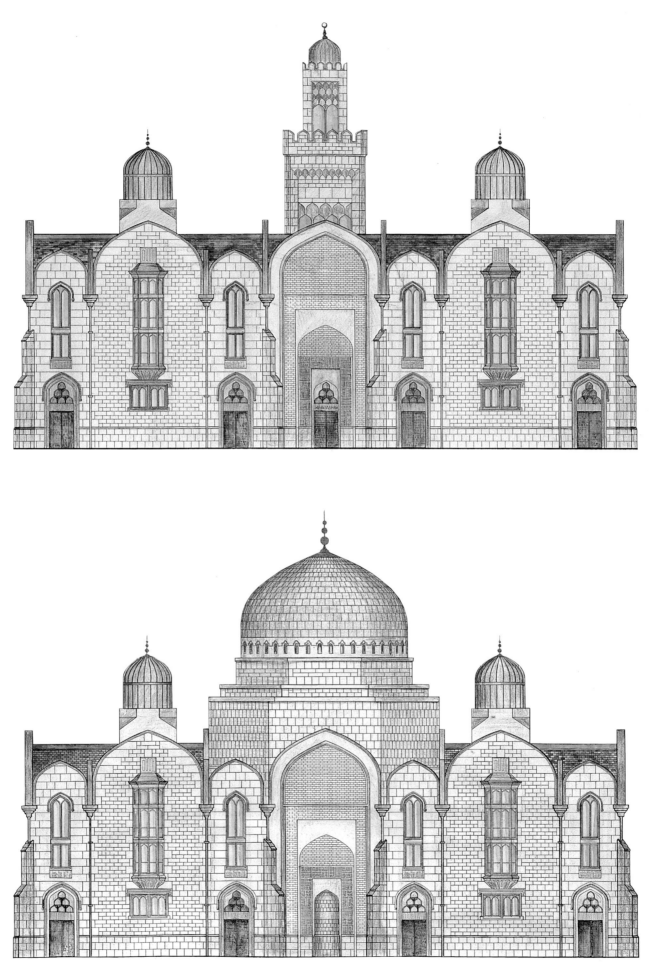

PREVIOUS PAGES: AERIAL VIEWS OF MODEL; *ABOVE:* FRONT AND BACK ELEVATIONS; *OPPOSITE:* CROSS SECTION SHOWING THE MOSQUE AND MINARET; SECOND PROPOSAL

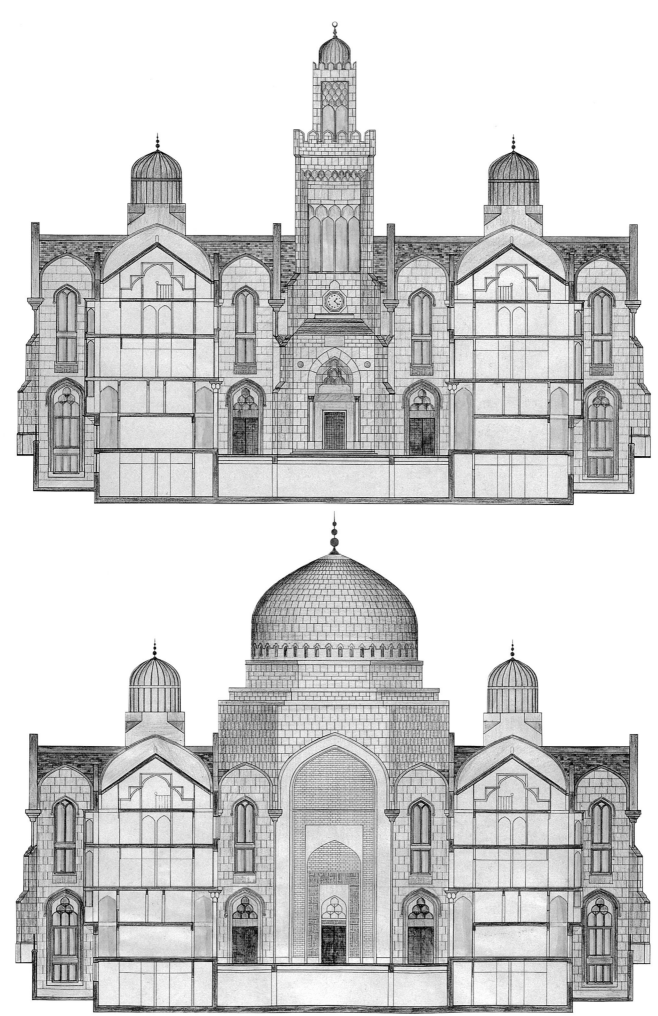

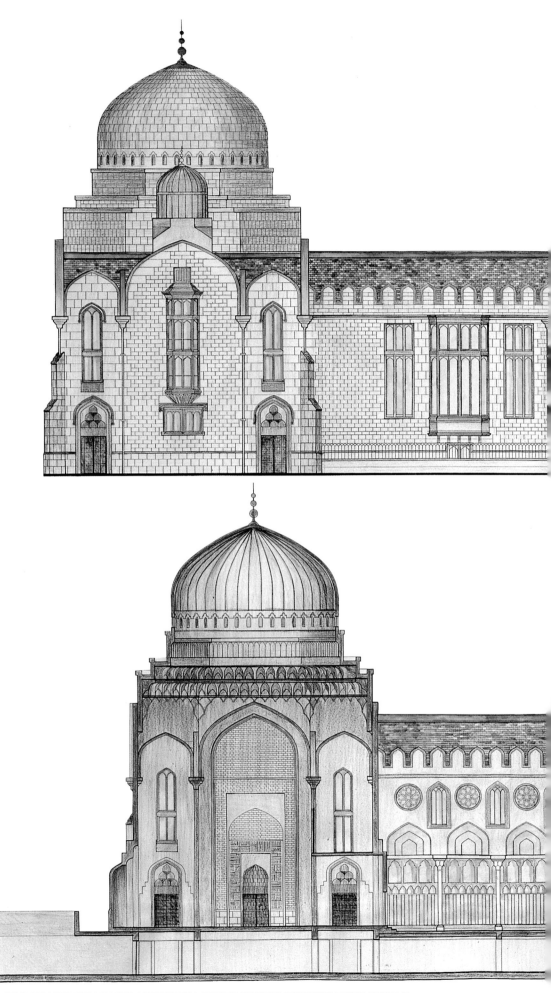

PREVIOUS PAGES: LOW VIEW OF MODEL; LONGITUDINAL SECTION AND ELEVATION OF THE SECOND PROPOSAL

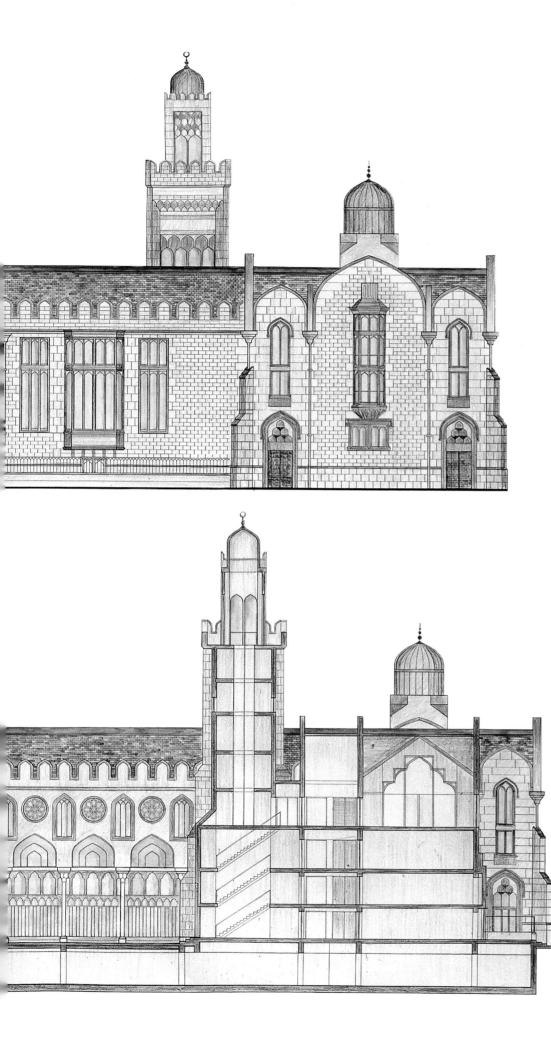

FISH CANNING FACTORY
TAIZ, YEMEN, 1991

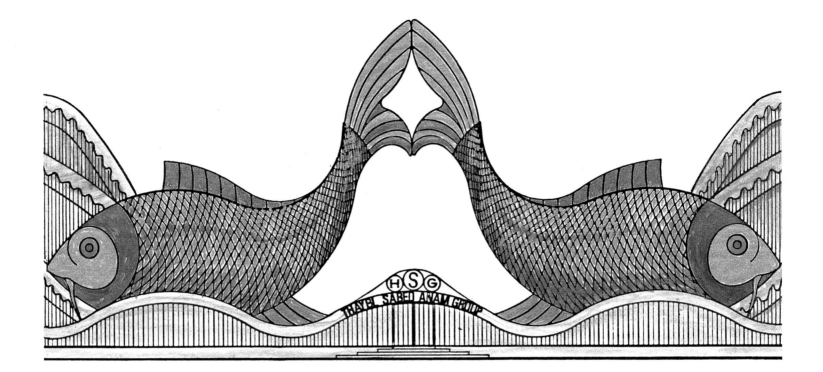

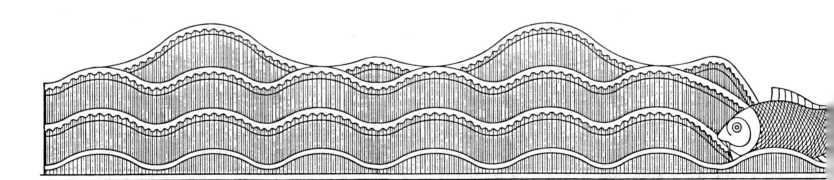

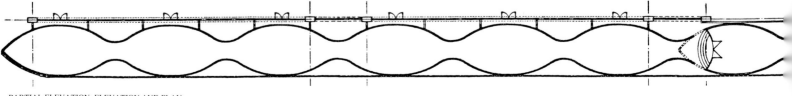

PARTIAL ELEVATION; ELEVATION AND PLAN

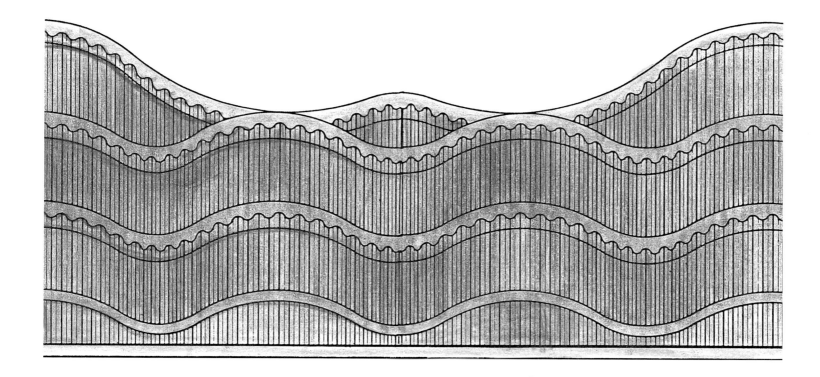

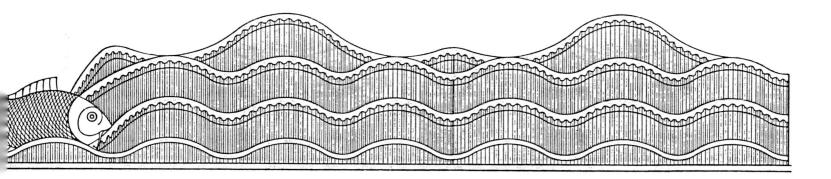

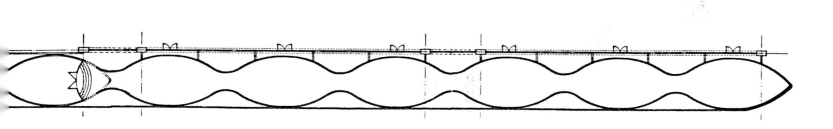

HOUSE IN LONDON SUBURB, 1992

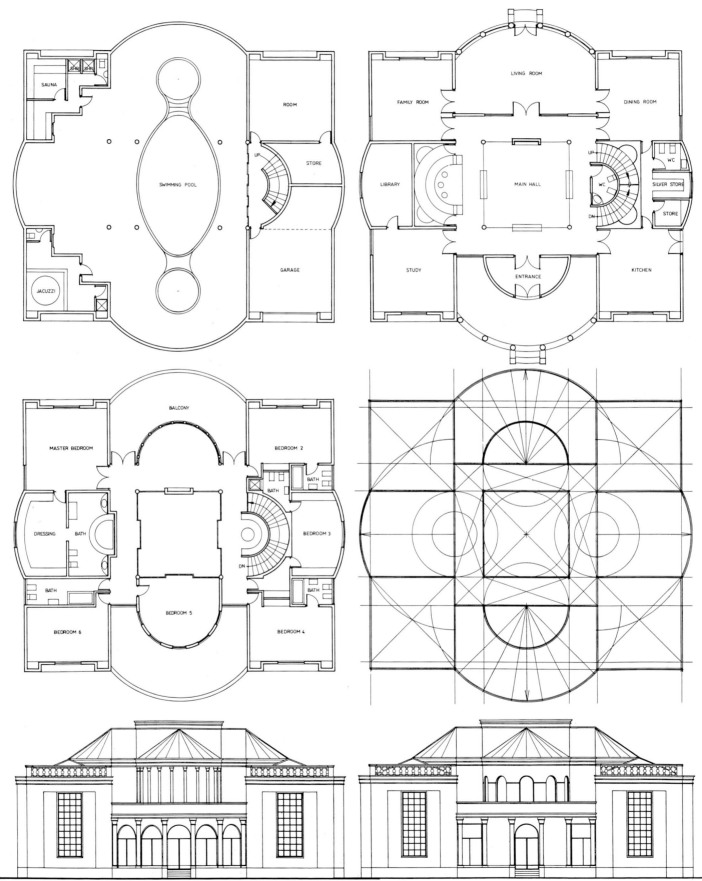

BASEMENT AND GROUND FLOOR PLANS; FIRST FLOOR AND STRUCTURAL PLANS; REAR AND FRONT ELEVATIONS

PRIVATE RESIDENCE
MUSCAT, OMAN, 1992

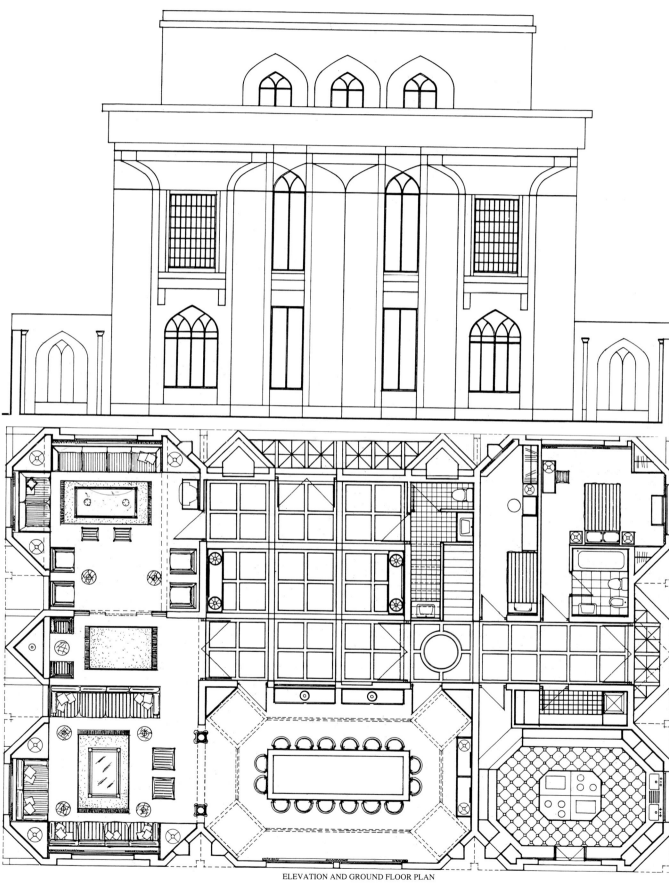

ELEVATION AND GROUND FLOOR PLAN

SHOPPING COMPLEX IN SOHAIR
OMAN, 1992

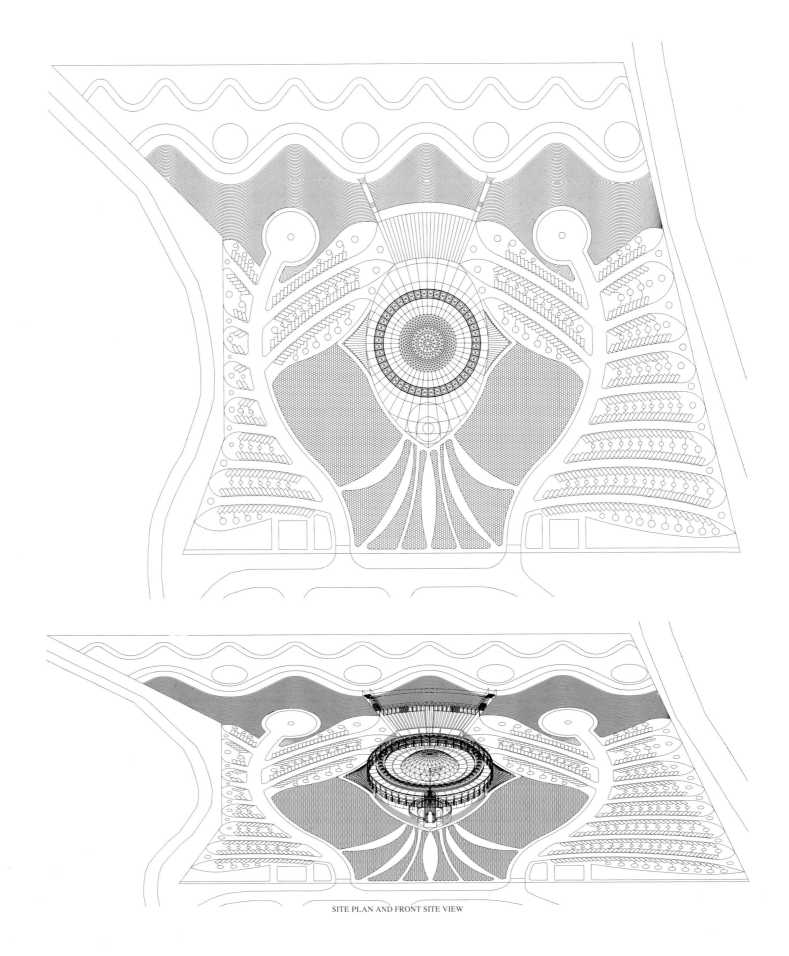

SITE PLAN AND FRONT SITE VIEW

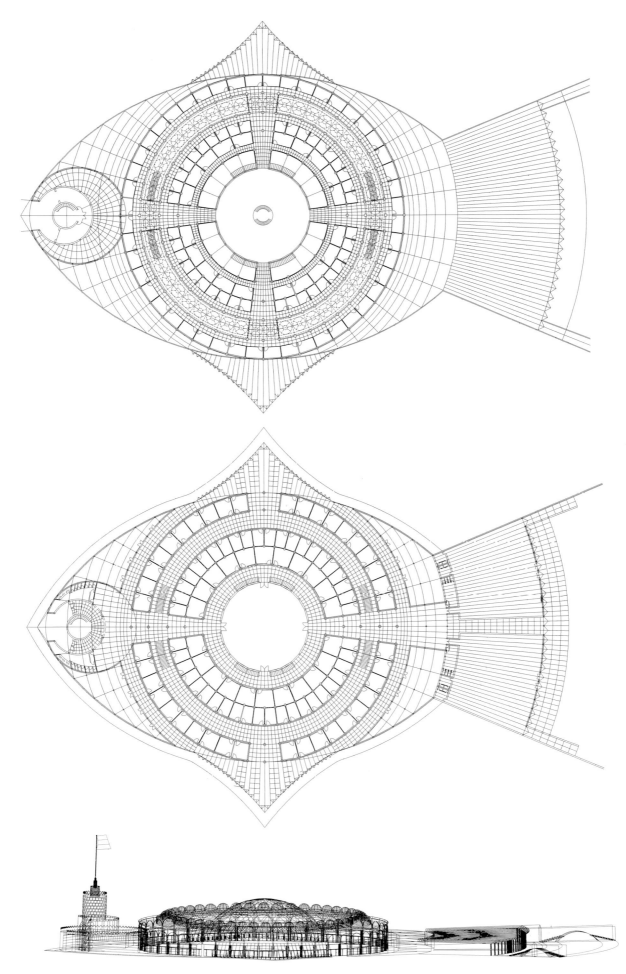

FIRST AND GROUND FLOOR PLANS AND PERSPECTIVE ELEVATION

CEDAR HOTEL
SIN EL FIL, LEBANON, 1992

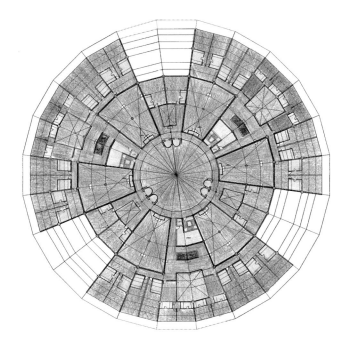

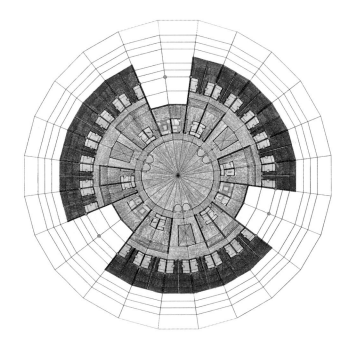

TWENTIETH AND TWENTY-SIXTH FLOOR PLANS; *OPPOSITE:* THIRTEENTH FLOOR PLAN AND SECTION;
FOLLOWING PAGES: GROUND FLOOR PLAN AND SECTION; FIRST, SECOND AND THIRD FLOOR PLANS

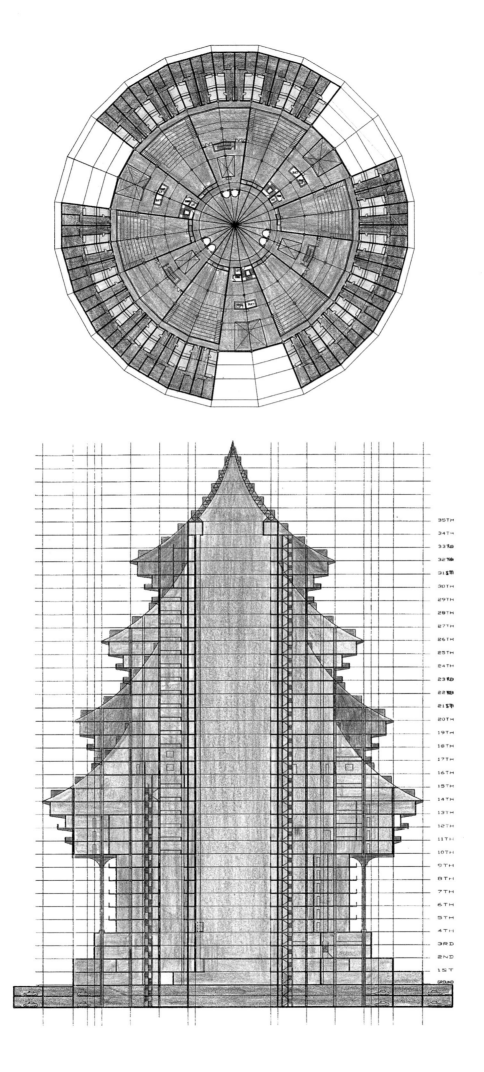

35TH
34TH
33RD
32ND
31ST
30TH
29TH
28TH
27TH
26TH
25TH
24TH
23RD
22ND
21ST
20TH
19TH
18TH
17TH
16TH
15TH
14TH
13TH
12TH
11TH
10TH
9TH
8TH
7TH
6TH
5TH
4TH
3RD
2ND
1ST
GROUND

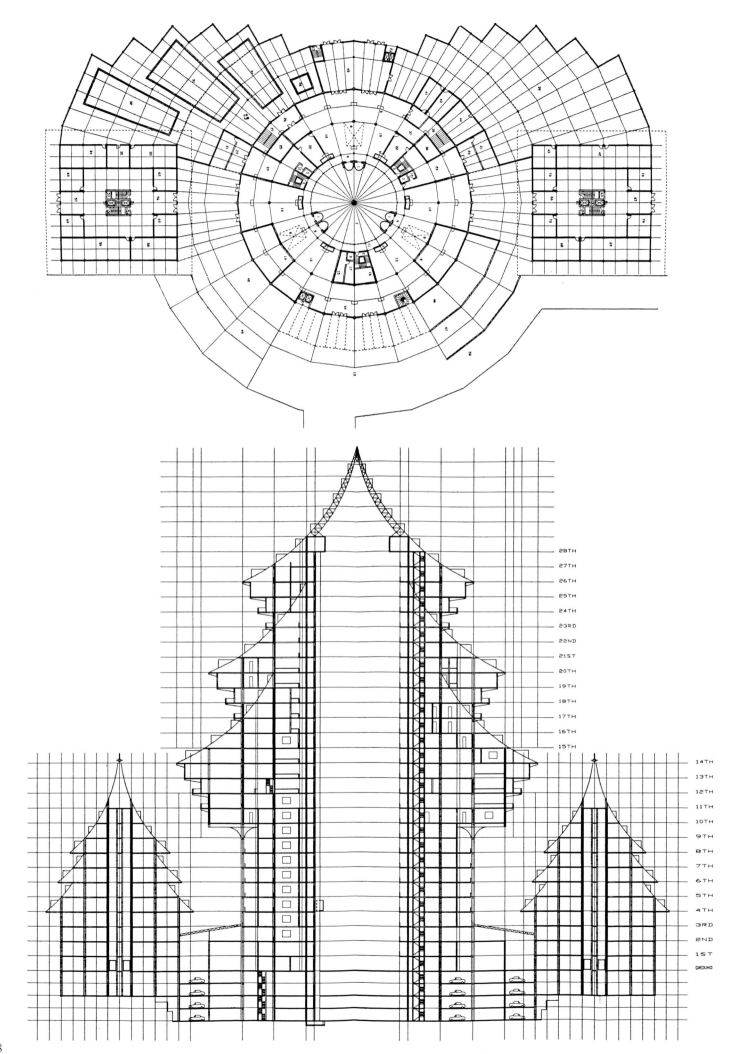

28TH
27TH
26TH
25TH
24TH
23RD
22ND
21ST
20TH
19TH
18TH
17TH
16TH
15TH
14TH
13TH
12TH
11TH
10TH
9TH
8TH
7TH
6TH
5TH
4TH
3RD
2ND
1ST
GROUND

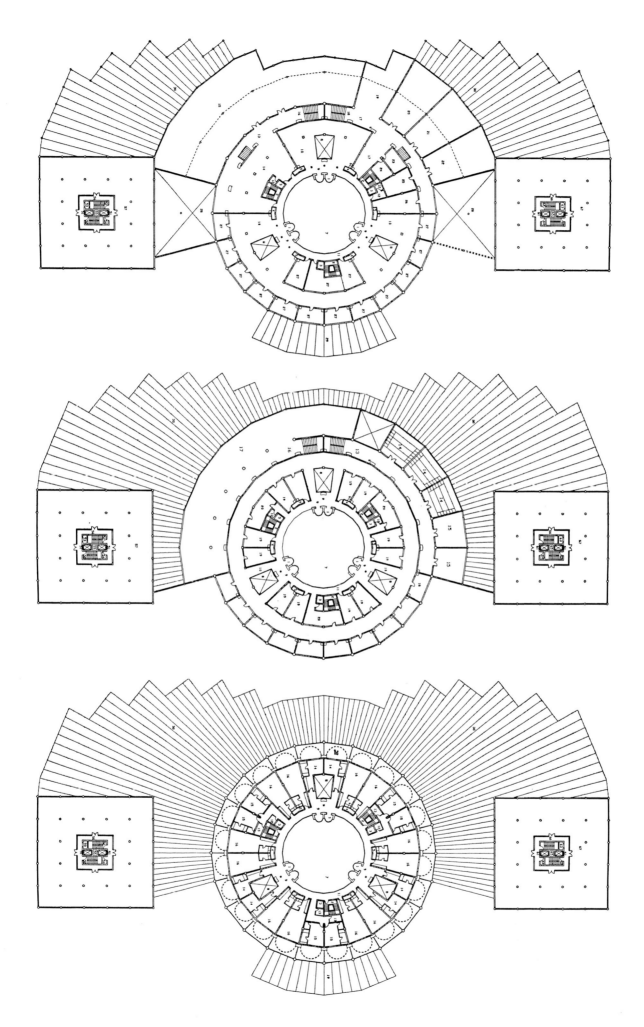

SEASIDE CHALET

JLAIAH, KUWAIT, 1992

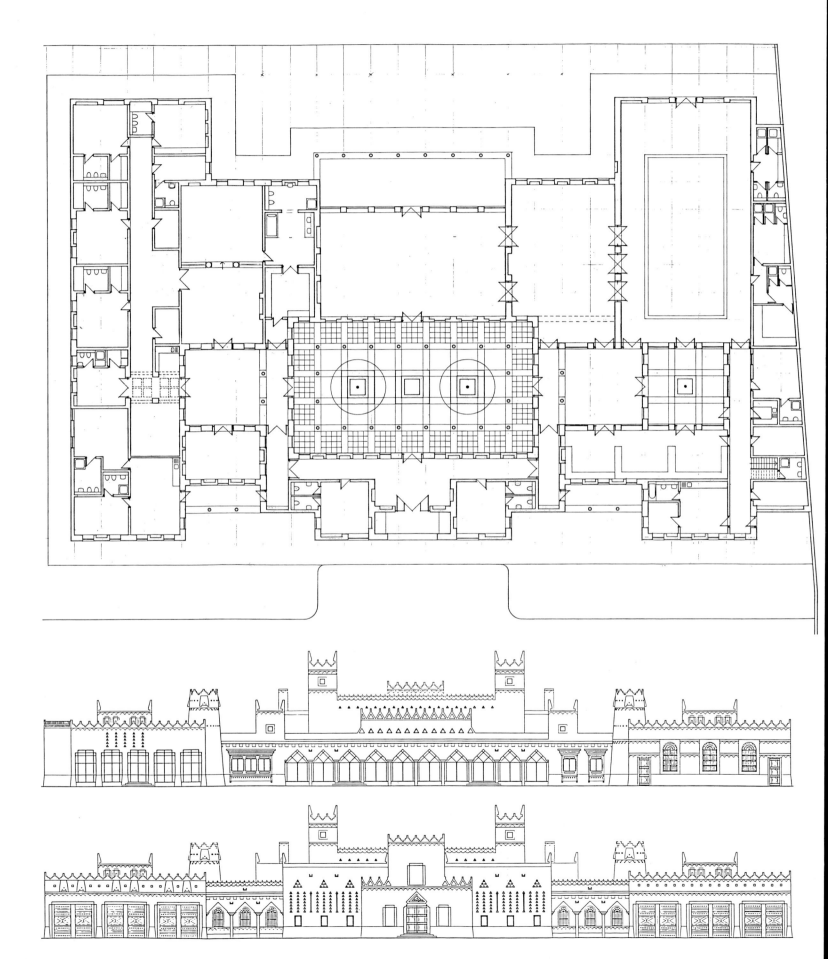

PRIVATE RESIDENCE
TAIZ, YEMEN, 1992

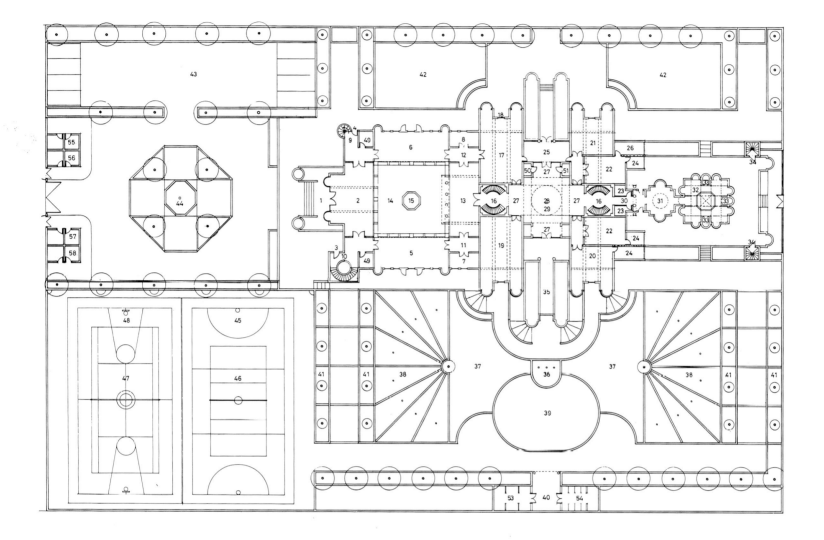

OPPOSITE: GROUND FLOOR PLAN; REAR AND FRONT ELEVATIONS; *ABOVE:* SITE AND GROUND FLOOR PLAN; GARDEN ELEVATION; GARDEN SECTION

SELECTED WRITINGS AND PUBLICATIONS

BY BASIL AL-BAYATI

Process and Patterns – Theory and Practice for Architectural Design in the Arab World, AARP, 1981

'Medina, Kingdom of Saudi Arabia', Paper presented at the symposium on the Arab city, its character and islamic cultural heritage, 1981

Community and Unity, Academy Editions, London, St Martin's Press, New York, 1983

The City and the Mosque, AARP, 1984

'The Mechansm of the Wasitah', *Basil Al-Bayati, Architect*, Academy Editions, London, St. Martin's Press, New York, 1988, pp 16-33

'Analogy in Architecture', *ibid*, pp 63-89

'The Hammam', *ibid*, pp 99-113

'The Relation of the Dome to the Ground Plan of the Mosque', *ibid*, pp 134-145

'Design for Islam', *Building Design*, 24 November 1989, pp 50-51

'Al Bahith An Al Horia Fe Al Mujtamaat Al Islamia' (in Arabic), *Alam Al Bena*, No 109, 1990, p 20

'Built for Islam', *Building Design*, 5 April 1991, p 24

ON BASIL AL-BAYATI

'Cultural Centre', *Architecture and Urbanism*, Tokyo, No 136, January 1983

'A Colloquium of Two Cultures', *Architectural Record*, February 1983, pp 53-55

'New Cultural Centre at Ad-Dariyata', *Al Benaa Magazine*, Vol 2 No 10, 1983, pp 7-9

'Revival in Islamic Architecture', *Ahlan Wasahlan Magazine*, Vol 7 No 6, September 1983, pp 15-17

'Analogy in Architecture in the Arab World', *Al Benaa Magazine*, Vol 2 No 12, 1985, pp 3-
'An Adventure in Islamic Architecture', *Ahlan Wasahlan Magazine*, Vol 9 No 11, November 1985, pp 30-33

'Contemporary Arab Architecture', *Mimar Magazine*, Vol 16, April-June 1985, pp 42-53

'A Future for the Past', *Middle East Construction*, Vol 10, October 1985, pp 31-35

'Basil Al-Bayati' (Interview), *Architectural Design*, Vol 56 No 12, 1986

'Towers in Islamic Architecture', *Arts and the Islamic World*, Vol 4 No 2, Autumn-Winter, 1986, pp 29-32

'Az Iszlam Muveszet Tortenete' (The History of the Arts of Islam), *Kepzomuveszeti Kiado*, Budapest, 1987, pp 276-543

'Protest Mars Ceremony', *Sunday Times*, 12 March 1989, p 1

'Art and Belief in the Mark of Basil Al-Bayati', *Asharq Al-Awsat* (the Arab International Daily Newspaper), Vol 382, 19 May 1989, p 11

Geza Fehervari, 'Faith in Tradition', *Building Design*, 9 June 1989, p 26

Frank A Walker, 'Eastern Promise with a Tartan Overlay', *The Scotsman*, 23 October 1989, p 11

Geza Fehervari, 'Back to Budapest', *Building Design*, 11 May 1990, p 34

Geza Fehervari, 'A Centre for Islamic Culture in Hungary', *Art and the Islamic World*, Vol 5 No 2, Summer 1990, pp 46-48

Michael Collins, 'Classicism in British Architecture', *Architectural Design*, Vol 59, 5-6 1989, p 58

Michael Collins, *Post-Modern Design*, Academy Editions, 1989, pp 242, 265, 288

'Function and Fantasy', *Architectural Design*, Vol 62, No 7-8, July-August 1992, p 88